A Voice Unheard

Poetry, Prose & More

Jan Toomer

Reality Undefined Publishing LLC

ISBN: 979-8-9866812-7-6

Cover by Jan Toomer

Contents

I dedicate this book to Alice Davenport who has been a wonderful supporter of New Mexico authors.

She has also been a source of information for many people due to her love of research over the years.

But to me, she was so much more; a friend with whom we both could let down our hair.

Thank you, Alice.

A Little Context

"It was unknown to
her how such grace
and beauty could
emerge from mere words."

I grew up with a mother with narcissistic tendencies (I don't believe she was formally diagnosed) and what would be considered an alcoholic today. And I was her "whipping boy" or girl in my case. It was also a time in the world where those who exhibited neurodivergent tendencies were regarded as lesser (though I don't think they had that terms/diagnosis back when I was a child, and I have never been diagnosed, so I may be wrong about me). Neurodivergent is, simplified, when one's brain functions differently than the accepted "norm". Yeah, kind of sucked back then.

I was also born a multi-talented sensitive which was very unwelcomed. I was born with many abilities already in place and working, such as Seeing the Other Side, including Seeing and Hearing the deceased and other types of beings. I was trying to live spiritually in a mundane world.

When I was taught how to read, a whole new realm opened up to me - the realm of words.

Then, probably around the age of ten, I discovered the joy of writing and playing with words. It was through this discovery that I found solace and an outlet from my fears, anger, loneliness, etc. of being the "Freak".

When I began writing for release, I wrote about my life, but also ventured into fantasy.

Many of my earliest writings aren't included – they were super corny, though I did try to include some of less cringey examples of my teen-aged corniness.

Since I was born with multiple abilities already active – hence my mother's enduring name for me, "Freak", because I didn't fit, or play well, in her desire to appear perfect with a perfect family – there are some writings that include what I've Seen (Other Sight), Saw and/or Felt as a child and teen, but made sure to not sound even more of the "Freak". I had learned early in life that anything I said would be used against me by my mother.

Growing up, I had access to woods, a lake, a pond and animals. This gave me a place to commune with nature and to rebalance. Nature made me feel safe, secure and able to just be me. I have often turned to nature and animals throughout my life. They were and are safe.

Later in life, my husband, kids and I lived in Germany for five years. It was here I took a course to refine my writing skills. One assignment was to write creatively about an actual event. I included this, *The Silent King,* in this book as well.

A friend pointed out that in my writings, a large portion of the themes or patterns are about experiencing falsehood and lies. I don't disagree. I am not looking for pity and do not consider myself a victim. I am merely sharing my perception of growing up in a society that wasn't welcoming to anyone different in any way.

The following entries spanned many decades and I didn't write consistently…only when I needed an outlet or felt moved to write. I eventually became a Metaphysical, Spiritual and Paranormal Consultant to aid others on their journey. So this book is basically a poetry and prose memoir of my inner thoughts as I progressed on my life journey as Jan.

Please be aware: this is not a straight-forward book of poetry, prose and short stories. Each entry includes some personal insights as to what it's about.

There are poems that were copyrighted under my now retired *Basics Course©* and *Undefined Reality©* course workbooks.

There are four of my poems that were published in National Library of Poetry (I retained all rights to my work): "Melody of War", 1996 in *Silence of Yesterday*; "Memories" (as "Untitled") in *A Muse to Follow*; "Immorality" in *Best Poems of 1997*; and "Silent Whispers" in 1998.

I also have some of these poems, and a little information about the poem, published on my website, Reality Undefined (metaphysic al-studies.com). These have been annotated appropriately. When needed, I added more information below some of these poems. And one poem, "Sometimes", was published in my book *Prophecy Revealed: Clarima Syd Jones*.

Hopefully my writings will bring hope; poke you; make you ponder; encourage you to ask questions in your life; or maybe just entertain you.

Thank you.

~ ~~ ~ ~~ ~ ~~

Human Life Experience

Living

Here I sit,
stoned again.
Learning bit by bit
that living is a sin.

Why I wonder
are we on this Earth?
I sit and ponder on
what is birth.

Birth is being born;
born unto this world.
Born to be scorned
of doing things unheard of.

Born to be a human being.
To hate and love as others.
In realizing and seeing;
you also have sisters and brothers.

You learn to love,
and you learn to obey –
the things above
all night and all day.

As you learn
living is a sin,
the passions begin to burn.
That's where is all begins.

So, there you sit
stoned again,
learning bit by bit
that living is a sin.

- --- -

I had been introduced to the now legal (in some states at the time of publication), herbal "weed". Since having a mother with narcissist tendencies, I was on constant high alert. Partaking of the "weed" helped my body to calm down, and I was able to think or See (using upper case for my Other Senses), which opened my world up quite a bit more, by helping to relax; a temporary relief from the constant fight or flight that I daily lived.

I pondered why we were here – as humans – if just about everything was considered a sin. I couldn't buy into it, nor could I understand it.

~ ~~ ~ ~~ ~

Ho-Hum

Ho-hum, school is a drag.
Every morning, say allegiance to
the flag.

Go to first hour; second and third –
The teachers are speaking; no one
has heard.

Go to fourth and fifth hour – finally the last.
Everyone is thinking of the future,
not of the past.

It's finally time for us to leave.
It's hard for some of us
to believe.

We're all going to home to rest for
the night.
We'll crawl into bed and stay out
of sight.

Starting with the rising of the sun,
the start of a school day has
once again begun.

Ho-hum, school is a drag…

– – –

I began experiencing pattern recognition. Patterns were, and are, all over our world and within our personal experiences. I saw this by mentally stepping back and observing the patterns of going to school and observing my and other student's energies throughout the day.

Yes, this is corny, but hey, I was in middle school. As I aged, I was able to expand in Seeing and understanding the patterns, and grow as a metaphysical, spiritual and paranormal consultant.

~ ~~ ~ ~~ ~

Man of 1000 Masks

Hiding behind the mask of a
thousand lies.
He can't tell the truth no matter how
hard he tries.
Or how about the one hiding behind
alcohol and pills?
Always finding new ways to get
cheap thrills.

Or the one hiding along with his
deceit?
Being nothing but one constant
big cheat.
Or the one with an ego the size of
a balloon.
When trying to find happiness – he finds
he is immune.

Or the one who hides behind
hatred –
despising the world; wishing them
all dead.

How about the man behind the mask of
a thousand lies?
Can you see through his
disguise?

- - -

Since learning about patterns in life, I began to watch people more – though this may have been a survival technique (gauging threats to my being as I learned to do because of my mother) – I noticed more about people.

And being able to read and interpret energy, I learned that my mother wasn't the only one who wore masks to try to hide her true self; I Saw and Felt it from peers and adults throughout my life. Some lied intentionally, and some were lying to themselves and possibly not consciously aware of doing so.

And I developed some masks trying to fit in – to appear "normal".

~ ~~ ~ ~~ ~

Man II

Think of man and the earth
he trods.
All of his falsehoods, beliefs
and his gods.
All the trees he's cut for warmth
by fires.
All the terrible things done to
quench his desires.

He has built the towers and
paved the roads.
Chased out the birds, and
squished the toads.

He has condemned the helpless;
scorned the well.
He has forgotten promises of heaven
and the threats of hell.
He is destroying this world
of ours.
Thinking of new ways; dreaming
of new powers.

He can't keep going like
this,
or the world will become barren, then
beauty we will all forever miss…

- - -

Speaking of patterns….another ability I experienced was being able to see the future of the timeline of what I was observing. I learned I could See (Other Sight) the most likely outcome of a situation at that moment. Unfortunately – and especially today – this projection of man hasn't changed.

~ ~~ ~ ~~ ~

The Road

The road is covered by the
mist of the unknown.
It keeps the outcome a
mystery to those who seek its end.

Maybe the road is the
road to knowledge;
to success, happiness.
Or maybe it leads to
destruction, pain or death.

So follow the road with
every precaution.
It may be eternal hell, or
the heavenly world of happiness and love.

You see, the road is the path
of life; the road to the unknown –
a mystery and
the answer hides beyond the mist.

- - -

Reality Undefined website: A vision showing me that we each have to choose our path in life.

- - -

This is speaking to each individual's journey or path. Some people I saw heading to peace and/or happiness. Some people were leaning towards self-misery and/or self-destruction.

~ ~~ ~ ~~ ~

The Silent King

His princely stance was contradicted by the short blonde hair bobbing in the wind and the deep set dimples that showed when he smiled. Studying the playground with fawn-like eyes, he wove his way towards the slide, occasionally pulling on his slightly baggy blue corduroys.

As he reached up to grab the ladder rungs, his royal blue flight jacket raised up, revealing a cumbersome belly. He climbed the ladder with his chubby hands straining to support the weight of his short, stocky body.

Triumphantly raising his fist, he claimed the large wood platform and adjoining slide as his domain. Children were scattered amongst the various wood contraptions on the playground, their laughter defying the cool wind and the darkening skies. His mother waved from a park bend and yelled, “Hello, Mikael!”

Mikael was watching the peaceful subjects below when he noticed an older boy entering his territory. As the tall invader strode towards the platform, Mikael took this as an open challenge. With confidence faltering, Mikael staggered. His eyes pleaded with the more experienced opponent, but the blue-eyed stranger’s determination did not waiver. Quickly, he closed in on Mikael.

As the challenger climbed the ladder, Mikael made his decision. Realizing there was only one way out, he leapt towards the slide, going down head first. His plump body landed with a thud in the sand pit. He dusted off his white Nike’s and looked up at the tower. The new king stomped his feet and shouted his triumph.

Mikael slowly rose, hung his head, and shuffled away from the slide.

- - -

The Silent King is a creative short story writing assignment through a course to refine my skills. We were living in Germany and I'd taken my children to a local park, and this is what I observed while sitting on a bench and watching children playing.

~ ~~ ~ ~~ ~

Melody of War

Caution: Disturbing Content

The conductor's hands work feverishly
as more components blend into the
hideous melody. Slowly, the
crescendo builds.

As it does, the cloud forms
over the earth, waiting…
Waiting for the note to signify
the apex of the concerto — where "it"
can strike the final chord.

When "its" chord is struck,
the unearthly wails of tortured
human minds and souls begin
their chorus.

Mutilated and mutated
bodies dance; the grotesque steps
become more staggered and
jumbled, until the music is no more.

And life ends
as we knew it….

So…this is war.

- - -

Reality Undefined website: I had just finished reading an article in a veteran's magazine about the atomic bombs – this verbal picture painted itself in my mind. (I often see what others are saying or writing.) I was told my guides wanted me to understand today's type of war. Sad and disturbing.

Published August 1996 in National Library of Poetry's *Silence of Yesterday*

\- - -

This one was disturbing to me. What I didn't share here was the understanding that these horrific wars really were orchestrated in real life – we just never got to see those who were the political-driven hidden conductors.

~ ~~ ~ ~~ ~

Time

When did I get wrinkles?
Where did the gray hair
Come from?
And what am I to do
With the remaining time?

- - -

I had actually developed a gray patch of hair at nineteen years old – just as my father had done. But, now, at age thirty, the grey hair had expanded and little crow's feet appeared at the corner of my eyes. This is when I realized that my body really was aging; I was aging. Our physical bodies are not immortal after all.

~ ~~ ~ ~~ ~

Where Are You?

Not physically –
but inside.
What do you think about
when you're quiet?
What makes you happy?
Sad? Afraid?
How much of what is said,
do you really hear?
Do you even know me?

- - -

I asked my hubby this often – before I found out that not everyone's internal monologues are twenty-four/seven. I was genuinely surprised to learn that many, if not most people, don't experience this.

I also often questioned how people thought – their internal monologues, songs and conversations. What was their process? What were their perceptions? What were they thinking about at that moment? Do they really know the one they're closest to?

~ ~~ ~ ~~ ~

Friendship

Have you ever crossed life's path
with one who you can:
sit comfortably, and say nothing?
Speak your mind, even if it sounds
ridiculous and they don't mind?
Balance your personality weaknesses,
as well as compliment it?
Be yourself?

Once in a while, Source brings
a very special friend into your life.
One so special that limited time
does not diminish the
quality of the friendship.

I've been touched in such a way –
And all that I can say is

Thank you.

- - -

I have been fortunate enough to have these special types of friends enter my life. They were rare and very precious to me.

The kind of relationship that months or years can pass, yet you can reach out to one another and talk as if no time has passed. I hope you, the reader, have had the joy of experiencing this type of friendship.

~ ~~ ~ ~~ ~

History Was Told

In man's early time, history
was told and retold, so as not to
be forgotten.

As man progressed, he
learned to honor and hear the elders.
For their wisdom and time earned knowledge
were indispensable.

Now, man, at his "pinnacle"
of evolution, has forgotten.

He's forgotten the wisdom the
Elders have to offer; the history
they've witnessed and the
knowledge they have learned.

- - -

Knowledge was passed down from Elders and knowledge was shared. Most of us have stepped away from that. And, generally speaking, in today's society, the Elders are deemed by many a drain and burden on the resources; feeble, and a bother instead of a resource. Today's disposable society; discarding the history and those who lived it, instead of learning from them.

I, ever since high school, gravitated towards the Elders. To hear of the history of them growing up in clapboard houses; of ice carriages dropping off blocks of ice for their refrigerator; the way they used to do things compared to today's modern conveniences. The Elders were, and are walking history and have so much to share...if only anyone cares to listen.

~ ~~ ~ ~~ ~

They Refuse To Leave

I tried to lose them –
running, twisting, hiding.
Yet they're still there.

I told them they are
not welcome – but they
never listen.

They demand my
attention and destroy
my peace.

They refuse to leave.

They came close once –
reminded me of a tornado
clearing a path.

I know what will
happen should I stop.
They'll catch me.

They will engulf my
soul – unforgiving flames,
consume and destroy.

Have they ever
followed you?

Their names are
Pain, Sorrow and Grief.

- - -

Reality Undefined website: The death of a loved one. As I grieved, I also watched those around me who grieved. I 'saw' their emotions as described in this entry.

- - -

Losing a loved one can create a myriad of emotions. And yes, I know firsthand. I've experienced a few losses, so I tried to capture grieving and how one may feel on this rollercoaster of emotions and turmoil.

~ ~~ ~ ~~ ~

Secrets

Some are large.
Some are small.
Some aren't' meant
to hurt at all.
Some are whispered,
some are angry,
some are smitten.
Some never were.
Some shouldn't be.
All hurt those
who love you and me.

- - -

I'm not sure how many people know this, but our energy fields show when we have secrets. The energy usually doesn't say what those secrets are, only that one has a secret or secrets.

~ ~~ ~ ~~ ~

Gen X

Grey hairs
surround the
no longer firm face.

Wisdom speaks
where rash
words once exited.

The walk more
confident - no longer
hesitant.

Ears clouded
from years of
loud rock.

Lines no longer
crisp, eyes see
beyond materialistic.

Yesterday's teen -
Today's parent -
Tomorrow's elder.
Where did time go?

- - -

Reality Undefined website: Variation on the "Maiden, Mother and Crone".

- - -

I am becoming (have become?) the Elder of my time. Will anyone seek my knowledge gained and wisdom earned? As it turns out, yes, some do seek me out.

~ ~~ ~ ~~ ~

Today

Once again the sun
peeks over the horizon.
Another day we've been
given to live.

How shall we spend
this glorious gift?

Spent behind a desk –
at a place that brings
misery to your soul?

Thoughts of bills
piling up – creditors
yelling "Past Due!"

Or fighting hundreds
for a ride on the
subway?

Spending an aggravating
hour in the checkout
line at the grocery store?

Or plotting to stay alive
on the freeway one more time?

Through all of this, when
will time be found to
watch clouds roll by?

Tell someone you
really love them?

Support someone who's hurting?

To be thankful for the
one more day we've
been given?

\- - -

I'm sure others have asked themselves if sitting behind a desk, working to pay bills, is what life's supposed to be like. So is it?

~ ~~ ~ ~~ ~

Windows to the Soul

Silver teardrops –
the only sign of
the internal agony –
hidden for so many years.

The full face smile
touches all – until
they see the eyes –
for there's no joy there.

If the eyes are the
Windows to the Soul –
and the eyes are vacant –
where has the soul retreated?

And why?

- - -

Reality Undefined website: This is when I realized a friend was really hurting within.

- - -

When paying attention, the eyes tells us about the person we are looking at. Smiles mean nothing unless they reach the eyes; the soul. Otherwise they are fake and it's an attempt to keep their pain and/or fear hidden.

~ ~~ ~ ~~ ~

Questions...

I've finally come to realize
that it is my nature to question.

Not necessarily doubt all;
but to constantly seek for the new.

To limit myself – to accept nothing
new – goes against that which I am.

I've also realized that I may never
receive all the answers in this lifetime.

But for me, to quit asking and seeking,
means to quit living.

And for that –
I am not ready.

\- - -

Reality Undefined website

\- - -

The theme of thinking throughout the night continued in this entry.

During my night time reflections, I realized that I had asked so many questions over my lifetime. I never hesitated, or hesitate, to ask, "Why?" This was a frustration for both my mother and my teachers when I was growing up. I still ask myself and others that question frequently. I mean...if you don't ask, you'll never receive an answer.

~ ~~ ~ ~~ ~

How Many

How many lifetimes
between now and tomorrow?

How many sorrows
and joys can we experience?

How many thoughts have
we created and let loose?

How many more horrors can man
create to do to man?

How many are ready to say
‘no more terror, war, hate’?

How many lifetimes
between now and tomorrow?

- - -

Reality Undefined website

- - -

Looking back, I felt like I’ve lived so many lifetimes in this current life...both the good and not so good. I’ve questioned how many other people lived multiple lifetimes in just this life.

~ ~~ ~ ~~ ~

Self-Proclaimed Princess

Her illusions jumble her vision;
reality just out of reach.
Her self-induced ignorance,
a cocoon of protection.

Her thoughts seem to be
“Others WILL take care of me!”

Self-appointed princess,
sitting atop her cloud throne,
dictating her wants to
a non-existent kingdom.

Her demeanor states
“I am above you ALL!”

Her words spin, a demand
tripping into a lie.
Another lie wrapped around her –
a smothering regal cloak.

Her words demand
“You will do as I SAY!”

You strip away her
traitorous cloak –
and she stands before
you, cowering.

Her eyes tell you,
“I hate you!”

And, for a brief instant,
reality sinks in…

she is the same as us –
and it scares her.

Her being says,
"Hold me! I'm scared!"

But only for an instant.
She immediately dons her
cloak, climbs to her throne
and re-activates her illusions.

And there she remains,
alone.

- - -

Reality Undefined website: I saw a lot of this behavior from some reincarnated Vietnam era soldiers who were angry at their treatment from their own government and people. There were also others who had reincarnated with a chip on their shoulder, thinking that everyone should bow down to them.

~ ~~ ~ ~~ ~

Facing the Abyss

As the day approaches
I become excited
for life as I've known
will cease to exist.

Like the fledgling which
stands at the edge and tests
his wings, preparing
to take off for the unknown…
so must I.

The fledgling faces his
new freedom, and his life.
And here I am,
completely clueless as to
what I'll be facing

As I stand at the
abyss of the unknown.
A smile on my face,
I leap forward
with open wings.

- - -

This is in the now retired *Undefined Reality* course workbook: Trusting in that which is beyond my knowing.

- - -

I was given the "Okay" by a dean at the local community college to teach my Undefined Reality metaphysical courses. I was terrified and exhilarated at the same time. And it did feel like I was diving off a cliff in an act of faith that it would go well. It did.

~ ~~ ~ ~~ ~

I Am Free

I took two steps and stopped.
Something inside my chest shifted…
then cracked and shattered.

I began crying…hard.

I tell God that I think I
just broke me…I'm broken
and that I don't know what
to do about it.

I feel as if someone grabbed me
and shook me, they'd
hear the broken pieces rattle
inside of me.

It was then I realized I wasn't
broken! I had just freed my
heart that I'd been protecting.
And I no longer needed to.

It was freedom I was experiencing…
not breakage.

I am free.

- - -

Reality Undefined website: Not sure what I was going through, but the feelings and experience were tangible. – – I remember the shattering of the remaining energetic cages I had built to protect my heart emotionally.

~ ~~ ~ ~~ ~

9/11

The Twin Towers had burned.
Men's minds became numb
as death tolls had mounted.

Then men's hearts burned with fury.

Has healing actually occurred,
or did we just make hearts
of stone?

– – –

Reality Undefined website: A blast from the past. My thoughts after the one year anniversary of 9/11.

- - -

Remembering when we watched what horrors, emotionally and physically, that occurred when we were betrayed by our own and the immense distress at the people we lost to the tragedy. Not only those who physically lost their lives, but also those who were deeply scarred by this atrocity.

It was after this that I never again celebrated Halloween; I could no longer light-heartedly celebrate death.

~ ~~ ~ ~~ ~

Deceiver

I promise you this ~
I dangle these promises in front of you,
and you blindly follow.

Waiting for the promised "secrets" all
while tangling your energy into
mine.

As you follow without question, I gain
more and more control over your energy,
your life.

It's feeding me and my insatiable appetite
for *more*; more followers, more
energy,

more *mine*; all while dangling, promising and
offering you mere tidbits….
if that.

Making you more dependent on me, for I control
the secrets that you want so
badly.

- - -

Reality Undefined website: This is the energy of the Deceivers.

Deceivers weave together their deceit, malice, control and fear – forgetting that they no longer need any of that – and then they "gift" this mix to those around them…but this "gift" comes with a very high price.

Subtle manipulation, all while the originator/deceiver wraps energetic bindings on the ones who accept the "gift".

An example could be someone who is a leader who manipulates others, especially through sometimes subtle fear tactics, to control them. Another example would be a narcissist.

This is the way of the Deceiver.

~ ~~ ~ ~~ ~

Deceiver Revealed

The words that were spoken
were farthest from truth –
masked behind a mantle
well-worn and bedraggled.

The deceiver began in a
frame of light – but soon was
to twist and darken, and then
hid it behind a smile.

The dark over ran –
the illusions broken –
the truth oozed into the room…
all took a step back.

Deceiver is alone – awaiting
new innocents, hoping
they won't take a look behind
the scenes of the twisted smile.

The dark could no longer hide –
the deceiver panicked –
"No one must know…no one
must suspect…"

Too late

Too late

Deceiver revealed.

- - -

Reality Undefined website

- - -

I watched as one who proclaimed to be a Lightworker chose the side of dark energy and continued to pretend to be of the Light.

Sometimes I'm offered an "assignment". This one was for me to be available and try to encourage – at the time – a somewhat prominent person within the spiritual/energetic community as she approached a crossroad in her life.

This person eventually – and a bit aggressively – accepted the darkness, but worked to keep it hidden behind a newly constructed façade of light.

My assignment ended when this person pretended to channel a being that never entered the energy around us. Instead, she pretended to channel and spoke of what she wanted for herself – complete control over others in her circle.

She had free will and had made her decision.

As always, the deception was revealed. She couldn't and can't hide from those who can See or Sense her true energy. I walked away.

~ ~~ ~ ~~ ~

Lost

The old – yet new to me – news
caught me off guard.

Why didn't anyone tell me?

Then I remembered…there was no one left
to tell me…he was the last.

I had closed and locked that door
a long time ago.

I started crying – realizing the enormity of this…
THERE ARE NO MORE.

Memories broke down the locked door –
memories of my daughter and borrowed son…

before they lost their innocence to
the drugs, alcohol and self-loathing;

before their anger…
and self-destruction.

One buried;
One behind bars.

Lost…so lost.

- - -

My daughter's suicide and my borrowed son – her best friend's descent into deep crimes and imprisonment left me saddened at their journeys that I wasn't able to redirect – though I tried. Even knowing it was their choices, their path, didn't make it any easier.

~ ~~ ~ ~~ ~

We Are the Zombies

I had a dream.
A restless dark dream.
A telling dream.

For years I begged
people to pay attention…

To take responsibility.

The words mainly unheard.

I had a dream…
a telling dream.

People ignored the horrors
building around them…

People waited for others
to fix the problems.

The others laugh
at all of us.

They say ***we*** are
oblivious and weak…

And they will do whatever
they want

to **US**.

I had a dream.

Oh God!

It wasn't a dream…

We are the zombies.

\- - -

Reality Undefined website: This really was a dream, explaining to me the "zombie" promotions from CDC (Center for Disease Control), and commercialization of "zombies" (games, movies, shows, cartoons, etc).

We are the zombies – made numb through various "carriers"; not thinking for ourselves. We can be herded and the body be destroyed from the inside out by chemical poisonings (GM foods, "vaccines", etc).

\- - -

We need to be pro-active in protecting our foods, our bodies; our children's bodies...our future.

~ ~~ ~ ~~ ~

There is No "Side"

I thought my stroke
had made it difficult
to "pick a side".

But that wasn't it.

I could, and can, See
both or multiple
sides.

Each opinion,
interpretation, and
even conspiracy

Is correct...

And wrong.

You see, it doesn't matter
either way.

Make a decision
and move forward...

And then it becomes your
truth – your reality.

Your reality may be
different from mine

and that's okay.

\- - -

This really showed up the during Covid years; the isolation and the fear-mongering was felt around the Earth.

Yet I saw beauty emerge as humans retreated. Nature breathed a sigh of relief and began working to rebuild itself.

People began looking within. Some it helped; some were terrified to look within.

This is when I really began seeing that each individual's perceptions and interpretations were 100% correct; for the particular individual. I saw that each "conspiracy" was actually real; and also had no merit.

Why? Because of each person's beliefs.

In this Earth matrix, our thoughts and beliefs make our individual realities. What may be true and real for you may not be for me. But each one is valid.

By stepping back and allowing each creator (person) the right to create their own reality, I can honor their path and honor my own as well, even if they go separate ways.

~ ~~ ~ ~~ ~

Death Experience

Immortality

Each passing day brings
the physical body closer to demise;
the soul closer to its Maker.

So what's left of us on Earth afterwards?
"Plenty!" I say.

Think about friendships you have shared,
strangers you have helped and smiles you have passed along.

Think about words of encouragement, counsel
and kindness you have freely given.

Think about memories you have built
with friends and loved ones.

What's left of you when you pass on?

Everything that has made you, YOU,
lives on in those that your life have touched.

Whoever said there's no such thing as immortality
was wrong.

We do live on.
Forever.

- - -

For a dear someone, to remind her – even if she didn't believe in reincarnation – we are still immortal. — Published National Library Poetry in 1996, *Best Poems of 1997*.

- - -

This was inspired by a conversation with my very much loved Grandma Rose. She asked me if I thought she'd made a difference in the world during her lifetime.

~ ~~ ~ ~~ ~

Ming

Her clear blue eyes
take a glossy sheen –
looking within and
seeing nothing external.

Her breath comes
harsh –
laboriously, keeping
self-alive by sheer will.

Age caught up with
her – stubbornness only,
kept her going.

But she's looking
inward now – and
sees not the loved
ones gathered at
her side.

One quick breath,
and she's gone.

Twenty years of her
friendship taken
away in an instant.

'Til we meet again…

\- - -

My blue-eyed, Seal Point/Himalayan mix Siamese cat named Ming.

I had originally picked her up from a breeder who was trying to dump the kittens because her Seal Point had snuck out and met with the neighbor's Himalayan; therefore, the kittens weren't "pure".

Never having owned a cat before, I didn't know driving her home to surprise my roommate for her birthday would bond the kitten to me. I was raised with dogs in the house.

I bathed Ming regularly because that's what I done with our dogs. Later I learned one shouldn't bathe a cat, but I continued to bathe her since we lived in Louisiana and we had no air conditioning. I bathed her to help her keep cool.

I had taught Ming to fetch, which she did all the time, until my now-husband commented in front of her that, "Cats don't fetch." She never fetched again.

She was with me for twenty years. I loved and now miss her.

~ ~~ ~ ~~ ~

Grandfather

A day does not pass
that you are not on my mind.
Your laughter dancing in my heart,
the twinkle in your eyes,
and the kindness and gentleness
given so freely through your love.

\- - -

My mother's father was known and loved by me on what felt like a cellular level.

My mother didn't allow us access to relatives very often, which made my time with my Grandpa all the more precious.

He and I would disappear into the basement while everyone else was upstairs. Sometimes I'd play in the old cleaned out coal chute and bin. Sometimes I'd sit and watch him work on his jigsaw puzzles and he always had music playing.

We rarely spoke – we didn't need to – our souls rejoiced just being near one another.

And I miss him dearly.

~ ~~ ~ ~~ ~

Grandmother

Your love is felt daily
making the miles between us
an illusion.

I treasure the wisdom you
shared with me – for I know
it was given from the heart.

I love you,
teacher, advisor, friend.

- - -

My father's mother, Grandma, whom I adored. Again, I rarely got to see her, but she was as important to me as was my maternal grandfather.

My grandma and I wrote letters to each other a lot. She was one shining light in the smothering darkness of my life with my mother.

When I was out on my own, Grandma and I wrote even more. And, as I healed and matured, I traveled to visit her in person every three months just to be with her.

After her death, she pops in now and again to chat with me.

~ ~~ ~ ~~ ~

Death Becomes Him

Twisting in pain and agony
fighting for breath as the
body slowly fails him.
Soul screaming for release
from its diseased prison.

A large gasp –
he stills.
Muscles relax and
the soul soars free.
Beauty returns in perfect peace.

Goodbye, Dad.

- - -

Watching energetically as his physical being was shutting down. Though my father-in-law, I always thought of him as my second Dad. I miss him.

~ ~~ ~ ~~ ~

A Slice of Cake and a Handful of Memories

Day after day, life was so normal.
You always had my back.
You were always there.
In my life; sharing my life.
And I shared yours.

But one day you weren't there.
A slice of cake you got for us
sat in the fridge.

The house became quiet.
And I was alone.

All that was left was a slice of cake
and a handful of memories.

But I'd rather have you.

- - -

Reality Undefined website: Don't take your partner or loved ones for granted. We don't know how much time we have with our physical expression on Earth.

Take the time to share that slice of cake, literally and/or metaphorically, before the opportunity is gone.

Have a life with no regrets.

~ ~~ ~ ~~ ~

She Knew

She knew that I knew
but she hoped that I didn't.

"No don't come, Mom. It's not a big deal."
She was going to be inducted into
the Phi Theta Kappa Honor Society.

She knew that I knew
but she hoped that I didn't.

Fear crept into her voice,
"I don't think I'll join after all, so
there's no need for you to come."

Any doubt was removed.
Unfortunately I knew,
despite her hope that I didn't.

"Join, don't join, it's okay.
We'll come see you and our friends."

Her voice a whimper, pleading.
"Mom, I don't want you to come."

I softened my voice,
"I know, but I'm coming."

I knew she was on heavy drugs again.
And now she knew that I knew.

Her mind screamed at me
"I don't want you to see me like this.
I don't want you to see I failed and
was on drugs again."

She knew that I knew.

We never made that trip.

We never saw her again.

About a week before we were to go,
she ended her life.

The drugs won.

- - -

Our daughter lost her long battle to drugs.

It's hard to watch your child self-destruct and nothing you did seemed to help; nothing seemed to stick.

She had started getting her life back on track, but even four hours away, I felt her re-emergence into the world of drugs.

And we miss her.

~ ~~ ~ ~~ ~

Life and Death

Life and Death are part of the cycle.

When our daughter was born,
it was a beautiful testament to life.

When our daughter killed herself,
that dark day…a testament to death.

It's up to each of us to make
those days in-between life and death…

…our best days.

- - -

As much as we don't like the idea of losing our loved ones to death, we will all die eventually; it's part of the cycle of being on Earth.

~ ~~ ~ ~~ ~

Mother

Love

Love is as fair as the summer rose.

It is a natural beauty from Mother Nature.
It is a happening of Father Time.
It brings happiness, joy and color
into the world.

It attracts the birds and the
butterflies and is always bright.
But, also like love, it has thorns.
And if you're not careful, one
gets hurt.

There are always way to patch
the hurt,
but the scar will always remain.

A rose, like love, is very beautiful;
but once it's separated from the
whole, it will soon wither and
perish.

One must always treat it with care
so it may always flourish with

beauty
throughout the years.

\- - -

When I was in high school, through trial and error and repeated attempts to get help, I realized that it didn't matter who I told about what was going on, no one would help me.

I left this poem for my mother to let her know I was done with getting hurt by her. I ran away. I boarded a bus to New Orleans. I felt so alone – ostracized within my own family, my school, my life. I felt I had no one to confide in or resonate with.

Thankfully, and fortunately, the bus driver had – unbeknownst to me – radioed ahead and had the police waiting for me at the next stop.

A few hours later, my father picked me up and drove me back home – in stone cold silence.

~ ~~ ~ ~~ ~

Runaways

A person who runs away from
reality is…
like a child afraid to sleep because
of green monsters under his bed.
Like a lizard that flees from the birds'
beak.
Like a hermit crab who hides in his
shell from unseen dangers.

A person who runs away from
reality…
because they love their parents,
whom they just can't seem to please.
Because they can't seem to
find themselves.

A person who runs away from
reality
is a person who wants to love and
be loved,
but doesn't know how.

So please help those who are
runaways,
for they need someone they can
talk to and trust.

- - -

After my thankfully short runaway experience, I began looking around me and discovered I wasn't the only one to feel like I did. Me being the "Freak" in other ways, outside of the typical teenager feeling like they don't fit in, I knew they weren't experiencing exactly what I was, but they were hurting nonetheless. I think this is when

I really started watching others – not in a creepy way; rather to understand the human condition.

In a sad way, this made me not feel so alone.

~ ~~ ~ ~~ ~

Sleep, Wake

Sleep
To rest your body.
Sleep
And be in peace.
Sleep
Let darkness reign over you.
Sleep
To forget your loneliness.

Wake
To work your body.
Wake
And be disturbed.
Wake
Let lightness reign over you.
Wake
To meet your loneliness once again.

- - -

How I felt each day was for me; being the black sheep of the family, and the whipping girl for my mother, made existence on Earth monotonous and just shy of unbearable.

~ ~~ ~ ~~ ~

The Sounds of Silence

The sound of silence
Rushing in my ears.

The sound of silence,
Something no else can hear.

The sound of silence,
I can feel it on my skin.

The sound of silence,
It's starting to begin.

The sound of silence,
Played in perfect harmony.

The sound of silence
Whispers, "No one can copy me."

The sound of silence
Is played uninterrupted.

The sound of silence,
A volcano of beauty just erupted.

The sound of silence,
It cannot be matched.

The sound of silence,
One becomes quickly attached.

The sound of silence
Will end very soon.

The sound of silence
Will leave with the moon.

The sound of silence
Is gone; perfect timing.

The sound of silence
Is gone; sun brightly shining.

The sound of silence
After the sun has gone down.

The sound of silence
Quiet around the town.

Then,

The sound of silence
Is rushing in my ears.

The sound of silence,
Something no one else can hear…

- - -

I don't know if it was my home environment, my excited connection to the Star People, or some combo, but I spent many nights unable to sleep.

I discovered there really is a sound of silence – at least to me – and it's a soothing whooshing sound.

At first I struggled to find sound in the dead of the night since my days were filled with sound. Oftentimes I would go to my room, close my door and listen to music to escape the noises and tensions at home. But night time, when the threats of my mother rested during her slumber, was wide open to me.

The sound of silence is very special to me, even all these years later.

~ ~~ ~ ~~ ~

Hopes and Dreams

Hopes and dreams were here –
now they're gone.
Like the rapid growth of a
newborn fawn.

- - -

Though I don't remember the specific event that led to me writing this, it was a common theme in life with my mother. I learned I couldn't trust my mother – though it's a trivial incident on its own, it is but one incident in a long stream of incidents.

One year my mother brought me shopping for Christmas. She said she wanted to get us some winter coats and she wanted me along to show her what I wanted.

It was when the poufy coats, which I really didn't care for, became popular. I looked at the different styles and colors and picked the perfect one for me; not only my favorite blue color, but it didn't have the quilted squares which I didn't like. Instead, it was smooth and straight. I was so excited that I could have a coat that was Jan-accepted and "peer accepted". Hey, I was a teen.

This was the first Christmas in many years that I was excited about. I eagerly opened my package containing my smooth, blue coat, only to find it was not the coat I picked out. This coat was a different color and was quilted. I watched as my sister opened hers…it was the coat I picked for myself.

This was a defining moment in my life. The culmination of incidents with my mother led up to this one coat incident. I never blamed my sister – she never knew what had transpired before she opened her package.

This was my wake up call. It was when I knew without a doubt that I was alone within my own family and house. There was absolutely nowhere for me.

~ ~~ ~ ~~ ~

Liar, Liar

Lies, lies and lies.
How can one live with all of those lies?
How can one spew forth nothing but lies?
How can one be trusted ever again?

Lies, lies and lies.
Does the liar not know what
they do to those they lie to?
Do they even care?

Lies, lies and lies.
Where and when did they learn
the art (?) of lying?
Why do they lie and cause pain?

Lies, lies and lies.
What does the liar feel when
they have lied to someone?
Does it matter if stranger or friend?

Lies, lies and lies.
Is it a power thing?
To lie and try to get by with it?
Is it an art of secrecy they're addicted to?

Liar, Liar
You cause so much pain
I think you do it to drive
all you know insane.
Is this how you thrive?

- - -

As a child, I first learned about lying from my mother. It started when she would barge into my room after an evening of drinking and tell me that she loved me. When she spoke the words, I Saw her energy blacken and twist. It took a while for me to understand what I was Seeing and Feeling. I was crushed when I understood that she was speaking falsehoods.

I grew up listening to the lies my mother told to me and others and this shaped me to despise lying. I soon understood that a person's energy severely changes when they lie. I wondered why people lied, and where they learned to lie.

When someone lies to me or to someone else near me, the liar's energy darkens and warps. This makes me physically feel sick to my stomach.

My husband tells me I am blatantly and sometimes brutally honest. This is why.

~ ~~ ~ ~~ ~

House of Horrors

Warning: Graphic

I always knew where my mother
was in the house.
My mother's energy felt like a fly
buzzing around a bloated corpse.

If my mother neared my bedroom — my sanctuary —
I'd feel the bile rise, wrenching my gut as if I
had witnessed that fly land in the
corpse's mouth.

Like a turtle popping its head out
of the water, so too my mother's energy
broke the surface, dragging the deep
depth horrors up with her.

I worked hard to keep my mother's
horrors away from my life, while my
mother worked to turn her own
daughter to the darkness.

It was years before I could break
free from the house of horrors
and its keeper – my mother – but
I did escape, and didn't look back.

Yes, the dark shadows dance
at the edge of my peripheral, but
those shadows fear
my light.

I am free.

- - -

Though I said I never looked back, that's not exactly true. I had to heal from this "relationship", and my memories keep resurfacing until I dealt with them.

In my mind, I can thank her now. Because of her and my experiences with her, I became stronger, more set within myself...so she was instrumental in helping me shape into the person I am today...and I like the me of today.

~ ~~ ~ ~~ ~

Red Dragon Lady

Why are you called that?
Why do you wear red?
Who are you, to keep
disturbing me?

Are you with Johnson?
Do you also wish to
contain that which you
have no right to gather?

Are you an Earth reality?
A symbol? A warning?

I feel your fear – yet
your desire to understand
that which you've not
yet touched.

Are you me?

- - -

Around this time, I kept Seeing a Red Dragon Lady. She appeared both as a human female wearing a deep red formal dress and as a deep red dragon. She would morph between dragon and human.

I was intrigued because Red Dragon Lady's energy felt familiar, but I couldn't pin-point whose energy signature it was.

I wasn't initially sure if the Red Dragon Lady was a darker aspect of me, or was it my mother? Over time and more interaction, I found it to be my mother.

"Johnson" was a nickname I gave to the dark entity that hovered outside the peripheral of my energy field. Johnson represented the darkness of humans…hate, wars, racism, etc. He was just plain evil; a tempter offering what he thought I wanted – if only I'd agree to work with or for him. A resounding "No," was my answer.

After unmasking Red Dragon Lady and closing the door on Johnson, the harassment and haunting from them ended.

~ ~~ ~ ~~ ~

Lost in the Dark

Alone, with my thoughts,
in the dark of the night.
My family lost in their
own beautiful dream worlds.

Then, I was given a glimpse
of 'her' pain.
I cried for her.

Her bitterness overshadowed
any happiness she might
have allowed herself.

When she sleeps, she dreams
not. She has made herself
forget how to…

For dreams remind her
that her fears and loneliness
engulfed all else.

How sad to be lost
in the dreamless dark,
alone.

- - -

Reality Undefined website: (See "Lost Dreams" for info.)

- - -

This and the next poem, *Lost Dreams*, were glimpses I was given about my mother. In my own anger towards her, I never really considered her as a person outside of my own experiences with her.

~ ~~ ~ ~~ ~

Lost Dreams

Once a shining star
for which you headed…
now a dim reminder
of what you have not.

Looking back, you weep.
Time was contradictive –
agonizingly slow – yet
the years sped by.

A hope for a once
naïve child, gone –
swallowed by adult
disappointments.

It's no wonder you've
forgotten how to smile –

You're the Keeper of
Lost Dreams.

\- - -

Reality Undefined website: This, and "Lost in the Dark" refer to the same person – and the understanding of 'her' (my mother) was given to me in the same evening.

~ ~~ ~ ~~ ~

How Can I Be Touched?

How can I be touched
by her pain and suffering?
How can empathy travel
along a barren path
which leads nowhere?

I've been told my mother
is very ill; suffering.
Yet it touches me not.
It's like hearing your
friend's mother's brother's wife is ill;
no connection to me.

Perhaps it sounds shallow;
perhaps heartless.
Is this where self-preservation
has led me?

I send thoughts & prayers
of healing, knowing they'll be
violently rejected; for her path
to me was barren shortly
after I entered this world.
If not before…

- - -

My Grandma Rose informed me that my mother was very ill; that specialists were brought from around the world, but they couldn't figure out what was going on with her. And I felt nothing. No connection.

Part of me felt guilty for not feeling anything; then concerned that I didn't feel anything. It was then that I realized that though I healed the energy from me to her, I had also removed myself, and my energy, from her.

I did send the healing light and prayers – but they were energetically vehemently rejected.

~ ~~ ~ ~~ ~

Military

How Many Lives

Doubt ripples within self.
Who to trust?
How much to tell, and to whom?
Lies surround me that aren't mine –
unwelcomed, unwanted.

Journals, poems, poetry
and prose
once again destroyed.

Decisions have been made.

Our marriage considered?
Trust violated forever?
How many lives must
I live as "Jan"?

- - -

It was hard while my husband was in the military and we were overseas. I always felt like I was walking on eggshells because of his clearance and my abilities – though the military had investigated me (part of my husband's the clearance process) and knew what I was.

A lot happened when my husband was away on assignments – things that the military did to me to make sure I knew they were in my life – like entering our home (off base) when I was out…but all of that is another story for another time. But this did cause a lot of stress and turmoil in my life.

At one point in my emotional turmoil, I destroyed all of my writings that weren't put away in storage. I didn't want the military to know more about me and my abilities without coming directly to me and asking.

And I battled myself about being myself.

Authenticity of self won out, which was a massive relief to me.

~ ~~ ~ ~~ ~

Lifesaver

Loneliness creeps in –
unnoticed at first –
until you feel you're
drowning.

In a room full of
people, yet feeling
totally alone.

Laughing and talking
on the outside;
crying and despair
inside.

Just relocated; spouse TDY *
or deployed.
Children in school.
Lifestyle, hormone or
attitude readjusting.

Does knowing the reason
make it any easier;
lessen the feeling?

Can someone toss me a
lifesaver?

- - -

I worked with several military volunteer organizations overseas. I also worked with the Family Advocacy and the Family Support Group.

I saw a lot of spouses adrift when overseas. They were far from home; their families.

I wrote this for them, to let them know that others have felt the way they feel – and that the Family Advocacy Support Group could help them.

** Temporary Duty – Soldier is assigned somewhere else for a shorter assignment and usually doesn't include bringing family members.*

~ ~~ ~ ~~ ~

I'm Home!

The black briefcases
stand in the corner,
collecting dust.

Fame and fortune
but a distant
memory now.

Long, frustrating
hours of work.
Own family awaits.

They once again have
a mother, a wife –
not a passing blur.

Is it worth giving
up money and notoriety
for my family?

Yes!

Why hadn't I thought
of it years ago?

– – –

We had moved from Germany back to the United States. At this point, because of the stroke, I couldn't work. A part of me – the workaholic that had been a contractor for the military – had died (but came back much later). I found I enjoyed being with my family more instead of being a blur in their lives.

~ ~~ ~ ~~ ~

Behind Closed Doors – The Cost of Defending Our Country

Soldier

I am afraid my nightmares will escape.
Afraid to sleep, for they may break the delicate barriers.
Sounds, sights, memories…unwelcome, unbidden.
How can I keep them from touching my family?
How can I remove the stain on my soul where evil had touched?
They are everywhere I run – until I can run no more.
They close in on me – fear, shame and that which remains un-named – shoved in my face.

Gasping for breath & tired…
tired of running from the fear and the sounds and images
burned into my brain – I retreat.
Life will never be the same.

Why can't they remain hidden?

Why do they haunt me?

They haunt me because it has become part of me…I am scared.

Spouse

When I look into his eyes – a stranger looks back.
I see a person haunted with painful experiences.
At night, I hear him stalking the corridors of his memories.
What does he seek, and why does it scare him?

I am afraid to touch the crumbling barrier he has
erected around him –
knowing it is delicate and soon to collapse.

What will emerge from behind that wall?
Perhaps the man I seem to have lost somewhere?
Since when does the cost of freedom mean not only lives –
but souls too?

I may never be able to understand – but I will love all of him
including the fear, and that which remains un-named –
for it is part of him.

I am scared.

Children

I don't understand. I know he has to leave for his job –
to make the country safe.
He is always gone. He has always come back.

But this time is different. His body is my dad's.
But he is different now.
He doesn't laugh anymore – and that scares me.
I don't think he knows himself. I don't know how to act around him,
and I don't know how to make it better.

I will hide, and maybe the problem will go away.

I am scared.

- - -

Reality Undefined website: This is why, especially on every veteran's day, I thank not only the soldiers and veterans but their families as well. For those who have no connection to the armed services, maybe this will give you a glimpse of what many service families go through.

- - -

Energetically observing the energy of a soldier, their spouse and the children; this is what it looks like from each person's point of view (energy-wise).

Soldiers don't always come back home complete; and some come back with extra...extra horrors, memories and new fears.

It's not easy being the soldier, the spouse or the children of a military member. It affects everyone.

~ ~~ ~ ~~ ~

Love

Spring is Here!

Ah! Spring is here
at last!
Winter's been temporarily
lost in the past.

The birds are singing;
grass is growing.
Leaves are turning green.
Flowers are showing.

The days are hot.
The nights are cool.
I enjoy every minute of it –
for I am not a fool.

The world is coming alive
with colors and with sounds.
It's becoming more beautiful
for the people and the hounds.

Everything looks beautiful
from where I rest.

I think this is the time
of the year I like the best.

Everything has beauty
and the grace of a dove.
Everything looks this
way because –

I am in love.

- - -

Again, I was a teenager, so some of my sappy and corny are also included.

As the animals became excited about the new growths, thus new opportunities, so, too, did I. And at this point, I have met my first love. I had written a lot tackier, dreamy-eyed stuff (which I'm not including). I wrote because this…being loved, being wanted, was so new to me that I cheesily gushed on paper.

~ ~~ ~ ~~ ~

Spring

The wind gently
whispers to us all.
It's reminding us it's
no longer fall.
The brook is babbling
hints to us, too.
Hinting to us why
the sky is blue.
The birds are singing to
us their harmonies,
Hiding in the branches
of the reborn trees.
The sun is beaming
with happiness.
Let's all try to make
the world shadowless.

- - -

A continuation of seeing Spring through the new-to-me eyes of someone experiencing love – okay, high school love, but still love.

~ ~~ ~ ~~ ~

My Secret

Some secrets are to be told;
some left to unfold.
Mine stay within me,
perhaps never to be free.

Love is being taught to me –
not how it was, but should be.
I have to break down the wall.
But what happens if I should fall?

He pushes me on relentlessly –
but pushes ever so gently.
As I fight through the dark,
to follow the song of the lark.

I know I'll push through this one,
as I have done before – and done, and done…
But when will the pain go?
It keeps hitting, blow after blow.

- - -

My first marriage, at a young age, I married a male version of my mother. I still had some trust issues to work through then. Unfortunately, my trust issues were not unwarranted. I eventually ended that abusive, narcissistic relationship.

It was with my current husband that I began to really learn what love was and is.

~ ~~ ~ ~~ ~

To Dad

Love –
Does it let you live in the shadows?
or does it destroy you by shattering
your illusions, just to show the truth?
I know not.

Seek.
Seek the truth.
Live in the shadows
of lies no longer.

Find me.
Hear me.
Seek the truth.

Sometimes our lies are
more comfortable to live in –
for truth does hurt.

But I, too, hurt,
seeing you live in
the shadows.

I am no hero –
but perhaps a fool…for letting
the lies build around us.

Perhaps I left it alone,
so I wouldn't bring
greater pain to you.

And I seek the truth;
some of which only you
can tell me.

Seek –
Seek out the truths –
Over thirty years' worth
as I do…

And perhaps we may
both be free…
from the shadows of lies.

- - -

I loved my dad dearly. He was a traveling salesman for liquid calibration metering (think gas pumps – those are calibrated liquid meters), so he was on the road a lot.

When I was nineteen and pregnant, I left home, desperate to get away from my mother.

Years later, after I had left my first husband and had remarried (and am still happily married for over thirty years), I had sent out an invitation to my parents; I wanted them to meet my husband and newborn daughter before we left to go overseas.

My mother called me to inform me that they would not be coming; she was furious that I had shown up alive on the levee. We previously ran into them while we were walking on the levee. I said "Hi!" to my father who did not recognize me and walked past me. I had lost a significant amount of weight during my pregnancy and didn't look like I had when he'd last seen me.

She informed me that she had told my dad that I had died. She said she had thrown away all the letters, invitations and announcements so my dad would never see them, because, after all, I was dead as far as he knew.

While we were overseas, I sent a registered letter to my dad. I begged him to reach out to me; to see and learn the truth (hence this poem).

I also wrote all that my mother had said she'd done. I apologized for not telling him sooner what had been going on all those years.

My mother had intercepted that letter.

For more on this, see my memoir: *Re-Writing My Future: A Stroke in Time*.

~ ~~ ~ ~~ ~

I Love You

Alone, each word means nothing.
Together, the meaning is so very special.
Alone, I feel nothingness.
With you, I feel whole.
I love you.
These are the hardest words
for me to say. Yet,
to say them to you is easy…
for it is the truth.

- - -

It took me a long time to feel safe enough to say those words freely; but learned I could do so without fear of rejection.

~ ~~ ~ ~~ ~

I’ve Searched

You don’t know how long
I’ve searched –
looking, seeking,
wondering if you really existed.

Then one day,
you entered my life,
and I knew that my search
was over.

Thank you
for your gentleness
and your love.

- - -

Reflecting on my husband coming into my life. I didn’t make it easy on him when he tried dating me, and later “wooing” me. My trust issues made the poor man work very hard…but it was so very worth it.

~ ~~ ~ ~~ ~

Strangers

Their eyes met –
hers defiant and angry.
His, a quiet curiosity.

Two stranger's paths cross,
and, in that brief moment,
two lives completely change.

His patient insistence
gently wears away
her lifelong barriers.

Coldness at his kindness;
he continues to seek a weakness –
one she refuses to show.

She demands he remain
nothing more than a stranger;
yet he quietly persists.

Her barrier, weakened in a moment
of self-reflection – he then speaks –
and shatters her illusion.

As her walls crumble, and
she is exposed, he moves closer.
Cautiously, she accepts.

They are no longer strangers.

- - -

Yeah, it's when I met my now husband thirty plus years ago. I really guarded myself and he ended up having to work hard to chip away at my multi-layered energetic brick walls of protection.

He won.

I'm glad.

~ ~~ ~ ~~ ~

Cats

Mischievousness
with fur.

Affection with
attitude.

Ever alert, yet
asleep.

I love cats!

- - -

Retired *Undefined Reality* course workbook

- - -

My view of my cats, who kept life interesting.

~ ~~ ~ ~~ ~

Stroke

Diagnosis: Death?

The question hangs heavy in
the air; echoes in my thoughts.

"Did you come home to die?"

I can't answer.

Oh, I want to – but refuse to
make a hasty reply –
for what if I'm wrong?

For the past three years
I've begged release from
the pain, the heavy sleepiness,
the anger and frustration.

HOPE a foreign word.

"Did I come home to die?"

I fear the answer – an
answer which evades me.
Probably by choice.

There are pros and cons
for either answer.

Perhaps I fear I've
no choice left but to die.

That is not my choice;
not my choice.

- - -

I still didn't know at this point that I had a stroke when overseas – I just knew something was very wrong and those doctors kept brushing me off.

By the time I wrote this entry, my body was shutting down; it could no longer bounce back and was exhausted from trying to keep going.

My husband found a doctor who listened. She asked me if I wanted to live. I decided I wanted to live.

It was over a decade of struggling to get my strength, memories (which didn't fully come back), and my abilities back – and to receive a diagnosis to explain what had happened to me.

It changed me forever – but I don't think in a bad way.

For more on this part of my journey, check out *Re-Writing My Future: A Stroke in Time.*

~ ~~ ~ ~~ ~

Unheard

I have a voice yet
remain unheard.
By my lover, my children.
I have worldly possessions,
and am thankful.
I have pets that exist,
finicky.
I am lucky.
I have a few special friends –
a blessing.
And my spirit screams
for peace.
I exist – I am.
But I have a voice
and remain unheard.

- - -

I begged doctors overseas to help me, but only received, “You’re walking and talking. You’re fine.” It wasn’t until over ten years later that I was diagnosed.

On top of that, we had moved back to the United States and I once again felt I had to hold a part of myself back because when I had let a little bit of the true me speak to others, my words fell on deaf ears or freaked people out.

When the words I spoke came true, then I became a pariah – like I had some kind of scary contagion. I was frustrated and confused. Aren’t we supposed to speak our truths? Aren’t we supposed to help others? It didn’t feel like it when I tried.

~ ~~ ~ ~~ ~

In the Dark of the Night

In the dark of the night
all are asleep…except her.
She stares up at the ceiling,
never feeling as alone as
at night.

Days are filled with sounds
as she does monotonous chores.
Every day. By herself.
No goal in sight beyond washing,
cleaning and cooking.

At night, as she stares into
nothingness, she wonders, “Why?”
Once life had a purpose – reason.
As always, her answer is the quiet
of the night.

- - -

Having gone from over ten simultaneous jobs – paid and volunteer – in Germany, to having a stroke and drifting aimlessly, was very difficult.

Before my stroke was diagnosed, I was unable to sleep most nights. We found out later that the stroke reversed my brain (sleep-mode in the daytime; wake-mode at night).

The long nights left me alone with very confusing and often disjointed thoughts and questions about my life.

~ ~~ ~ ~~ ~

Hypothyroidism

The doctors ignored my pleas for help
as the fat in my body went haywire
and I could no longer think clearly
nor stay awake all day.

They said the medicine was definitely
not causing all of these problems.
Stress, they said.
No one believed me.

The days turned into years;
the pounds and inches grew.
I tried dieting, starving, and exercising.
I could actually feel the fat producing.

I was no longer me, but I knew not
what I was, nor who.
I finally gave up and started preparing
for my death. I knew it couldn't be far.

I accepted the fact that I wouldn't
receive any help. The military doctors
couldn't and wouldn't admit there was
a problem – and they had made it.

Fifty pounds later, a civilian doctor
was found. Hundreds of dollars later,
she confirmed – there was a major
health problem.

By the time I met with her, my body
began shutting down. I could no longer
digest food. It just sat there, no matter what
I did or didn't consume.

I couldn't make it twenty minutes fresh out of
a night's rest without being exhausted.
I cried out of anger, fear and frustration.
I was dying, and alone.

Test results showed that my glands had
gone haywire. No hormones worked as they
should. The body was shutting down, and
was exhausted from the years of battling.

Never in my life had I been so huge,
and so scared. I detest this body I've
become trapped in, and pray that the
hormones will quickly settle so the fat will die.

I look in the mirror and do not recognize the
fat blob before me. The doctor reassures me
that nothing I'd done to lose weight would've
helped. Have patience.

How many people in the world
have had their lives destroyed, their bodies
destroyed or forever screwed up by a doctor
who didn't give a damn about what they've done?

I no longer have any faith in any human.
Too many lies, falsehoods, pain.
Shame on me for believing in anyone –
only believe in Source and self.

- - -

I was exhausted, scared, and really ticked off. Unfortunately, all the years of the doctor prescribed corticosteroids, like cortisone and prednisone, didn't help piled on top of my still unknown stroke. I had lost faith in all Western Medicine and military doctors.

I took my husband outside and told him I was dying and that I had taken out a large life insurance policy since the military doctors kept recording that nothing was wrong with me.

He asked me to give him some time to find someone to help me. He found a wonderful civilian doctor for me that discovered my body was shutting down. We still didn't know about the stroke, but this wonderful doctor was able to help me to keep me going in the meantime. I'd have strong, coherent days, but mostly I was lost in a daze or a haze. This civilian doctor was able to provide support and aid me in having more coherent days; but I never knew when the haze might re-appear.

Over ten years after my stroke, I was finally diagnosed. We realized I'd never had hypothyroidism; a stroke is what I had.

~ ~~ ~ ~~ ~

Hormonal Rollercoaster

I understand you never
know when you'll ride it.
Men and women suddenly
find themselves on it.

Have you ridden the
Hormonal Rollercoaster?
I hear the bigger one
is worse than the teen one.

Tears flow uninvited –
Then life looks grand.
Anger spews forth
for unknown reasons,
while sleep begs eternal.

- - -

Yes, both men and women go on the rollercoaster ride. I had gone through menopause four times, starting not long after my stroke. Each time I experienced different menopause "symptoms" – thankfully not all at once. Most people only experience it once and many sail through it.

For men, it's generally labeled as "Mid-Life Crisis".

~ ~~ ~ ~~ ~

Mystic Warrior

What is it I'm not seeing?

Why am I so empty?

What am I supposed to do?

This dried up Mystic Warrior.

I dream of yesterday's battles won;

of yester-years accomplishments;

of past goals.

Are all of my goals accomplished?

So where do I go now?

And will I ever dream of tomorrow?

– – –

Reality Undefined website: I had lost, and was beginning to re-build my abilities.

I still could not dream or receive visions at this point – and the 'novelty' of experiencing life without abilities had long worn off.

As it turns out, I had left behind the Mystic Warrior (which is why the reminiscing) to go on to some pretty cool stuff!

- - -

I really I had no purpose, no direction. The stroke had also rendered me unable to focus for many years.

For more on my stroke and how I was able to heal, emotionally and physically, please check out my book, *Re-Writing My Future: A Stroke in Time*.

~ ~~ ~ ~~ ~

Where Does One Look?

Dawn creeps over the horizon,
the night once again over.
Meanwhile, my spirit
drifts on, lost.

An end is near, but I
know not what is
drawing to a close.
I seek –

A mourning process in progress –
unknown to me what loss
I grieve – too many
variables.

Once again, I ask –
Where does one look
when you're not sure
what you've lost?

- - -

My conscious mind was unpredictable. I had lost a lot of long term memories (and short term memory retention really sucked until I began retraining it).

The stroke, and the partial reversal of the stroke, still left me with a hole. I didn't, and don't know what used to be located in that parts of my brain that were affected by the stroke, but I knew (and know) there are many missing pieces…but don't know what they are.

I asked my Team of guides about the large amount of missing data from my past; will I ever get them back?

The answer was an absolute, "No".

I asked why. They explained that the memories that were missing were not needed. For me to move forward, those memories were removed.

Perhaps you can't really miss what's gone if you don't know what is gone; you just know "something" is missing and grieve its loss.

~ ~~ ~ ~~ ~

Song of Beauty

The melody of crickets
transforms the night air.

Human sounds
Laid to rest.

The silent song of beauty
Performs here nightly.

It is not something heard –
Rather felt, sensed and known.

And enjoyed.

- - -

One of the rare days that I was consciously aware, and on that day, I could see the beauty of life around me.

As I began seeing the beauty of life again, I realized I might not be "stuck" anymore.

~ ~~ ~ ~~ ~

Cheddar Sunshine

Here I sit, munching,
On orange square crackers;
reminiscing of days past.

Little bursts of noisy joy,
followed by quiet, as
everyone stops to reload.

Filling and satisfying,
bringing a twinkle to the
eye fills the heart.

Alone, the quiet is
smothering – and the
taste not so sweet.

And I reminisce about…

A few Cheese Nips
between friends.

- - -

This was one bright spot on my stroke journey. A friend and I decided to go to the gym to work out at least once a week to help us work out our frustrations in life.

This was followed by an unhealthy but tasty ritual afterwards…eating cheese crackers with my friend.

~ ~~ ~ ~~ ~

Rejoice!

To BE again!
The colors, pictures
feelings and smells!

The sweetness of
beyond's touch.
Indescribable beauty.

To feel sounds –
smell essences –
to hear the unheard.

To dream the unknown –
the gift of ages;
to see the unseen.

Rejoice Angels!
Rejoice with me!

For I am me again!

- - -

Reality Undefined website: My abilities begin to re-appear (after my stroke and coma). Sporadically at first, but eventually grew and stabilized. I began to feel more like 'me' again. I know, it's a bit corny!

~ ~~ ~ ~~ ~

Nature

Silent Whispers

In the cool, quiet evening
the wind whispers to the trees,
revealing not to us its secrets.

The trees, after learning the wind's secret,
drops subtle hints to the ground,
like colorful leaves in the crisp fall.

The birds, also knowing the wind's
secret, has left behind them the
bare trees and darkening skies.

The birds have all disappeared;
they have flown in the opposite direction
from whence they came.

And soon, the wind's secret will be
revealed, when the wintery-white
blanket covers the land so it
may sleep.

- - -

Published by National Library of Poetry, 1998.

This began my earnest writing for release; not an escape, rather an outlet. I turned back to nature and tried to capture with words what I was seeing and experiencing. I also watched people with healthy relationships, which I hoped to experience one day.

~ ~~ ~ ~~ ~

Fall

The first few hints of fall
are showing.
The flowers are hibernating;
the grass is not growing.

The leaves are turning to bright
colors, golden and red.
“Oh, how beautiful!” are the thoughts
running through my head.

The squirrels are busy gathering
their acorns.
When they bark and chatter, I smile
to myself; I do not scorn.

The days are growing shorter
than before.
Nature is preparing for winter,
this we cannot ignore.

The nights are getting cool
and sharp,
but I love it so very much, so
you shan’t hear me harp.

- - -

I was once again turning to nature to soothe my soul. Watching the changes in the weather and the animals reacting to the weather changes fascinated me and helped balance me. It was nature; it was natural. And it all felt right. It quieted the unease of my home life.

~ ~~ ~ ~~ ~

Memories

I sit on the bank with
my feet in the water.
Memories nibbling on my toes.

The water sparkles
like diamonds
in the sunlight.

The wind caresses
the land so gently.

Frogs bellow with joy,
as the butterflies
dance on the breeze.

So, this is life.

– – –

Published as "Untitled" in *A Muse to Follow*, NLP 1995.

- - -

Water is a wonderful healer. As a child, I spent as much of my free time as possible either in water or near water.

As an adult, my joy at just putting my feet in a body of water is delightful.

I did, and do, also enjoy seeing the water beings dance on the water...making the water sparkle like diamonds.

~ ~~ ~ ~~ ~

My Temporary Home

An explosion of color
from earth's palette;
Its artist created
beautiful elaborate
painted landscapes.

Steeped in history,
both honorific and horrible;
past and present co-existing.
Teaching and learning.

Arizonians cactus-tough,
Earth-wise; yet, gentle
and giving people.
Southwest civilization.

The sun striking –
drying, reddening, heat.
Cool evenings, caressing –
Healing sun's harshness.
Never ending cycle.

The heavy rains come,
virtually drowning all
in its path,
atoning for its year
long absence?

The night time winds
lull you to deep sleep;
Then re-arrange your

outside furniture for a
morning surprise.

And I, but a visitor, am
enjoying the grace and
harsh elegance of such
a beautiful world
unto itself.

- - -

Reality Undefined website: We came to Arizona when we came back from living overseas. What a shock to me! The terrain and so-called seasons were so foreign to me. But, as time went on, I realized the fun and beauty the Southwest offers.

- - -

When my husband was driving us out to his new post, we drove for miles through brown…well, everything. The mountains were brown; the grass (if you could call it that) was brown; the scrub brush was brown.

I looked over to my husband and asked, "Where in the *bleep* are you taking me?"

I ended up loving the desert and discovered there is a lot of life in what I initially thought was barren lands.

~ ~~ ~ ~~ ~

Planet Earth

Stars shining bright
eternally optimistic –
or perhaps uncaring –
twinkling incessantly.

Waves bashing
to and fro –
never tiring –
sometimes with vengeance.

Sun spreading heat –
rays seek all.
Growth and death
rolled into one.

Moon waxing and waning,
month after month.
Not knowing its
power held over earth.

Wind, gentle and strong.
In temperamental fits
of caressing and
twisted destruction.

Man cannot change these
to fit him.

- - -

Reality Undefined website: A lesson on mankind's desire to control everything.

- - -

The last line was a warning, but man has done it anyway. Mother Earth is not happy.

~ ~~ ~ ~~ ~

Progress?

The song of the crickets
fill the night air
while birds hide amongst
tree branches.

The creatures of the night
come out, skirting the
edges of man-made lights.

All are seeking that
which man has consumed…

Their homes.

- - -

Since I spent nights awake and alert, I would focus on what was available to my consciousness at that time…the dark of the night, literally and figuratively.

~ ~~ ~ ~~ ~

Mother Earth

The sky is monotone.
My vision is blurred by the heavens tears,
which fall relentlessly into puddles
of sorrow unobserved.

Can you not hear my
thundering cries?
Can you not see my
flashes of anger?
Can you not feel me tremble
and quake with fear?

Do you not see my blood
erupting from my open wounds?
Do you not feel my breath
become heavy and polluted?

Can you not feel me
dying?

Help me.

– – –

Retired *Basics Course workbook*

- - -

Mother Earth's pleas became much louder, so I wrote what I was feeling from her.

~ ~~ ~ ~~ ~

Winter

The blanket of snow
was laid across the landscape.

A reverent hush
fell over the land.

It is time.

The snow signaled
the purification.

The past erased for
the new to begin soon.

We bundle for the
rest of the winter

knowing the new
will come in spring.

– –

I've always loved seeing new snow blanketing the Earth. Its purity and its peace, like the land is slumbering underneath this blanket to gain strength for Spring.

~ ~~ ~ ~~ ~

Misc.

Born and Raised

I was born and raised a Northerner,

and taught to speak proper.

I was brought to Louisiana,

and they said, “That won’t stop her.”

- -

I was beginning to explore more of myself and the world – sometimes through the lenses of humor.

~ ~~ ~ ~~ ~

Untitled One

Strangers in the night.

Unseen by the human eye.

Stars are shining bright,

as the wind gently blows by…

- - -

This just flitted through my mind in one of those rare moments when I could be still.

~ ~~ ~ ~~ ~

Her World of Fantasy

Welcome to the World
of Fantasy,
where things aren't really
as they should be.

The skies are gold; trees are pink
and the grass is blue.
You know everyone, but
not one knows you.

Everyone is so very happy – they
laugh and they smile –
The land is like that
mile after mile.

Where is this World of Fantasy?
Beyond the trees and the sky.
The reason for its existence?
No one seems to know why.

It is a land of peace and
tranquility.
Maybe this is the way it
ought to be.

There is no reason to speak
when you have something to say.
No one knows the year, the
month or even the day.

The land is unique in its
own strange little way.

After being here once, you
might even want to stay.

Wake up, Susie. Snap out of it,
right now!
I can't have you staring off – I was
talking to you, anyhow.

You needed help, so you came
to us.
Will you please sit still? And quit
making such a fuss.

Now, you've got to stay with reality – you
keep leaving time and time again.
Susie? Listen to me – when you will you
listen, Susie? When?

"I cannot," thought Susie, "let my
world become a has been –
I think I shall leave reality and
join my world again…"

You're not different here; everyone's
the same.
We're all alike – but we've each
a different name.

"Oh! I do love it here! I shall
never, ever leave!
Why, oh why, can't those in reality
just believe?"

Susie? Susie! Will you listen
to me?
"No, no! Please just leave
me be!"

"Oh, I do wish others could
see my world here.
Then everyone would be happy,
and nothing to fear."

"I do wish the doctor would
stay out of my business.
I think I shall go and just
leave my mailing address."

Please, Herr Doctor, I think
I shall go.
Yes, if anything comes up, I'll
let you know.

Hello, World of Fantasy! I
am back!
Yes, I got rid of that
ridiculous quack.

It is so peaceful here, full of
tranquility.
I have decided to leave
the World of Reality.

So here I am, I shall
never ever leave.
To hell, I say, with those
who don't believe.

Doctor! Doctor! A message about
Susie, our patient.
The landlord found her comatose
when he went to collect the rent.

Well, Doctor, I guess she is
happy –

having left our world – the one
of reality.

Yes, George, she is so very
happy –
now that she's forever in the
World of Fantasy.

\- - -

This one is pure fantasy…or is it?

I've been able to See other dimensions or realities off and on throughout my life.

I had memories of such a place – and a vague sense of being very much in peace, as well as in harmony with nature – but it wasn't on Earth.

This story played out in my mind of a female who withdrew from Reality. But, I ask you, which realm is really real?

~ ~~ ~ ~~ ~

Not a Dream

If I opened my eyes
Could I see him lying by me?
Could I reach out and touch?
Can it be a dream?

How many times have I seen him
lying there beside me?
How many times have I heard him
whispering my name?

I opened my eyes –
No longer could I see him.
Can I be asleep?
Can it be a dream?

Yesterday he left me
standing there alone.
He said it just isn't working,
for me to try it on my own.

All alone.
On my own, Lord.

How can I make it out in the world
so alone?

It's been months
since he left me.
Yesterday he called on me;
came to see how I was doing
out there on my own
so alone.

As he turned to leave, he said
he was happy out on his own.

No.
No.

Lord, it's not a dream.

- - -

During my first marriage, I was up late one night. There was a contest to write lyrics to the music provided, so in the dark of the night, I let the music guide me to the words – and this is what I came up with. No, I didn't win the contest, but I did enjoy the creative process.

~ ~~ ~ ~~ ~

Flu

Nose runnin’

Eyes itchin’

Throat burnin’

Stomach turnin’

Fever risin’

Flu here agin.

- - -

Again, tongue-in-cheek. I was not amused to see that the flu was making its annual circuit through the city again. So, why not poke fun at it?

~ ~~ ~ ~~ ~

Shadow

When a shadow cries,
can you see its tears?
Can a shadow love,
or know past from future?
Is a shadow evil, since
it reflects no color?
And where does it go,
when you die?

- - -

I watched my child's shadow when she was outside playing on the playground, and this is where my thoughts went.

~ ~~ ~ ~~ ~

THE PEARLY GATES

The gates stood before him, guarding what lay beyond.

He'd come so far, and in a seemingly short time.

He saw no one in sight to let him in, so he pushed.

The gates wouldn't budge.

His mind protested, "But they're supposed to be open!"

No one ever said the gates would be locked.

Of course, no one said they wouldn't…

– – –

Retired *Undefined Reality* course workbook

– – –

Just a little play on reaching the "Pearly Gates" only to find them closed and locked.

~ ~~ ~ ~~ ~

Metaphysical 1

Sacred Eagle

My wings have grown tired
and become tattered from non-stop flight.
I tuck them neatly away,
as I stand on the high tree branch.

I have flown long and hard –
through many storms and pleasant times.
But now it is time to rest, for I have grown
so very weary.

As I sit perched – I observe below, and
am very bewildered.
What has happened to those below
while I traveled abroad finding my path?

All around I see unfaltering confusion.
Do they know not where they're going?
And why do they look lost in their own realities?
Do they not realize; do they not see?
We've only one reality –

Life.

As I sit pondering, I see an older and more
tattered one approaching.

As the old one lights beside me, I see he
Is more weary than I.

I ask him why he flies on – has he not yet
found his path?

He smiled and replied…
"Yes, young one – but now I fly to guide."

And with that, his smile broadened, and
the old one once again took flight.

With renewed inner warmth, I gained
new strength to continue.

I silently thanked "Life",
stretched my wings, and soared.

- - -

This is the first time I wrote about what my Team of guides had said when they answered my question.

I told my Team I was worn out in the realm of humans and asked, "How much more do I need to endure? What am I even doing here?"

This poem is what they showed me.

~ ~~ ~ ~~ ~

Steps

You were a seeker,
and sought.

Now as a student,
will be taught.

Then be a teacher,
to another guide.

Then a master,
with all inside.

Let it be known
to all the above –

You are bound to
Light and Love.

If any of you
should go astray.

A debt incurred –
be immediate to pay.

– – –

Reality Undefined website: This was explaining to me the cycle we each go through – sometimes repeatedly within one lifetime.

- - -

Yep, we cycle through these steps again and again within each lifetime. Patterns and cycles are all throughout out our lives.

~ ~~ ~ ~~ ~

Who is Really Writing?

As if in trance, she watches
the pen in her hand
creating written beauty
on the page.

Words flow forth;
pen caresses paper
from her hand, yet
separate from her.

She wonders how
the magical dance is
done, since she has
no conscious control.

Hand and pen waltzes
to unknown music.
Thoughts and emotions
coming to life.

Animated without her
mind interacting.
How can this be?
Decidedly an outside force.

As quickly as it began,
the magic stops.
Or had it?
She reads what is written.

It was unknown to
her how such grace
and beauty could
emerge from mere words.

She realized that
though the dance
had stopped – the magic
continues to live.

– – –

Reality Undefined website: Oftentimes, "I" would write things that I had no idea where they came from – as though the writings were directed by someone else. I wonder if I had done automatic writing without realizing it. (Not what I recommend.)

- - -

I began my business and started my blog to offer stories, insights, experiences, etc. to those feeling alone or ostracized for being energetically different, energetically or otherwise.

My articles are written with my Team of guides so that whomever reads it may get what they need out of it.

Though I don't do automatic writing (it's my body, thank you), I do Hear/Sense my Team. I can See thoughts, words, sentences, that can flow from the ether down into my head and down to my hand. My Team and I work together to write.

Because I "dial" in to a higher frequency, I rarely remember what I've written, even if it's my own experience that I shared.

~ ~~ ~ ~~ ~

Life

The blood red moon
foreboding against the
black velvet sky.
Unobserved by many.

Merkaba effortlessly
glides above – un-noticed –
third dimension dwellings.
Ignorance self-induced.

Training continues –
wonders never cease.
Previously known –
recently re-introduced.

A new beginning starts
before the old ends.
Too much knowledge
to be retained in present.

Going back to gather,
piece by piece –
slowly released back
into the consciousness.

When all remembered,
and honored –
the final journey –
we transcend.

– – –

Reality Undefined website: My awareness and abilities are beginning to re-grow.

- - -

As my abilities began resurfacing and grow, information would flood in to me, but I needed some time for my brain to process and make it available to my conscious mind. This information often came in visuals or like a short story playing out in my mind's eye.

~ ~~ ~ ~~ ~

GateKeeper

GateKeeper, GateKeeper,
guardian of the door –
Let me pass through –
back to Nevermore.

Keeper of the Secrets
lend me the key.
I need to find, to know –
the real me.

Time Master, set me
free – let me go –
to fly ‘twixt and ‘tween –
forever flow.

Master of self –
both low and high –
All of the above is
simply in “I”!

– – –

Reality Undefined website: We each individually decide when our abilities, and which ones, we will use in this life.

- - -

There really isn’t an energetic external GateKeeper. It is, and always has been, self. This is the information that this dream experience imparted to me.

I believe that we can learn while we sleep. Sometimes my teachings come in story form; sometimes in what looks like written form within the dream or vision; and sometimes in prose form.

~ ~~ ~ ~~ ~

The Magic Calls

The magic calls to me –
teasing, begging to be used....

Just touch it, just once to dance
with it – to join with it.

Not so easy – because you then
want to dance

and dance with it more and more
and when you do....

you become less and less human
and more and more magic.

It's alluring, the power and potential
it holds.

I've heard stories of people who have
gone too far, who have been consumed
by the magic, never to return.

But I can't help but be drawn in
by the promise of power, and the
potential for greatness.

So, I take the risk, I take the plunge
and I embrace the magic.

At first it's overwhelming, as I explore
the depths of the power and potential.

But slowly and surely, I learn how to
control it, how to wield it,
how to use it and shape it.

The magic has become a part of me,
and I have become a part of it.

It has changed me, and I have changed
it.

We are one – the magic and I.

And I wouldn't have it any other way.

- - -

I had learned to fear my abilities, my "magic", by my mother's words and actions towards me and my abilities. I eventually understood that my abilities were – and are – part of me; not to be feared, but rather embraced.

~ ~~ ~ ~~ ~

I Was Once Called Mother Earth

I hear the stars call out my name –
while Mother Earth speaks her tales of woe.

My heart aches for mankind's cruelties –
my soul wants to fly free once again.

I see the many possible paths man has
created for their lives and Earth's.
None of those possibilities are any that
I wish to be around to witness.

I am Watcher and Listener – only
occasionally – and briefly – a doer.

I sit in an imperfect body – battered
and destroyed by trusting others to care for it.

Am I to cripple the rest of the way?
A battle to survive? And for what?

To witness man's cruelty to man –
Man's destruction of Mother Earth?

I was once called "Mother Earth"

Maimed, polluted, weary, trapped;
wishing to once again reach the
stars uninhibited.

- - -

Seriously, I was given the nickname "Mother Earth" in my young adulthood. Those who gifted me that name did so because I could feel Mother Earth's pain, and hear her pleas for help from what man was doing to her. I also knew when earthquakes were beginning to build, even though, at the time, I didn't live in an "active" area.

~ ~~ ~ ~~ ~

The Watcher

Content Warning

I see death and destruction –
natural and man-made.
Earth against human;
brother against brother;
husband against wife.

Years before it actually
happens; I see their fears.
Thousands of deaths
echo in my head.

Little heard were the
warnings; the pleas
to change the ways
of today.

I am the Watcher.

And I see…

The sweet innocence
still etched on the
child's face; trusting
even as he was brutally
murdered.

- - -

Retired *Undefined Reality* course workbook

- - -

This one was hard for me. Being an empath, whether it's one person or the people of the world…I would get moments of Feeling and Seeing what one or more people were experiencing. Empaths feel other's emotions as though they belonged to the empath. But it's not just humans we feel; some of us Feel animals, plants, and Mother Earth.

~ ~~ ~ ~~ ~

Believe

You go on, day after day,
doing the mundane in your world.
One day, your peripheral vision
catches movement.
You stop, turn your head and look.

A shadow freezes, then dissolves
into the background.
You see nothing, shake your
head and move on.
Once more, uninhibited, the shadow
is free to dance.

If you don't believe, how
can the shadow become a reality
in your world, and share with
you the joyous dance of
life?

- - -

Retired *Undefined Reality* course workbook

- - -

Our peripheral vision sees much more than, and beyond, the mundane visual reality. And our peripheral can see the movement of the Other…until we turn to look straight at it.

As we grew up, our forward vision was trained to only see the physical; while our peripheral was forgotten. The peripheral can catch movement that is just outside of our physical realm.

~ ~~ ~ ~~ ~

Reality Not Defined

Know it is within,
all past, present and
future.

One time line,
spiraling.

Touch beginning
and ending in
one breath.

No separation –
no singular "self" –
so many.

Dreams hold many
keys – reality not
defined.

Therefore, there are
no limitations.

- - -

Retired *Undefined Reality* course workbook

- - -

This is the basis of my business, Reality Undefined LLC, and of the now retired course and booklet *Undefined Reality*.

Nothing in reality is defined until you – each individual – create it.

~ ~~ ~ ~~ ~

HELP WANTED:

Need Guardian Angel for additional support. Experience preferred in handling a human who is sometimes a bit over curious; believes anything is possible; will dig into any dark corner and sees life as an adventure to be lived to its fullest; in other words, a handful. Only those willing to not doze off or turn their backs for a moment need apply. Shift work and plenty of overtime available. See Cassie's overworked G.A. for applications.

- - -

Retired *Undefined Reality* course workbook

- - -

My fun thoughts of what my Guardian Angel (G.A.) must have gone through – and is going through – watching over me. Though I was kidding, I appreciated my Team of guides in my life.

~ ~~ ~ ~~ ~

I Am the GateKeeper

GateKeeper, GateKeeper
Give me the Key!
We came and went before you –
Why couldn't you let it be?

- Bringing across death and anger
- As you came and went
- Balance and harmony a must
- Unbalanced by your malcontent.

To destroy you and your hold,
GateKeeper this I say.
Will free the portals, and
Leave me to my own way.

- The gate and key are
- One within me
- Kill me and you'll
- Still never be free.

- My body may die
- And flesh may rot;
- But I am the key,
- Body or not.

- - -

Reality Undefined website : I had a dream of closing and locking a portal (wormhole) – stopping some negative entities from coming back to Earth.

- - -

A dream where some nasties (typed in italics in the poem) wanted me to open a portal to let them through to Earth; and my responses. For as long as I can remember, I have Heard requests from the Other

Side in my dreamtime to open the portals and let them "in". It's has always been a firm, "No," from me.

~ ~~ ~ ~~ ~

Music Dance

Pan flute calls the innermost depths of your soul.
Bass tempts your body's rhythm, while woodwinds weave through the dark recesses of your mind – leaving nothing hidden.

A spring breeze swirls around you, lifting you to join the magical dance of the music.
Smell of morning dew penetrates your being.
Participating beyond the known five senses, awakening some you never knew you possessed.

Choral supplies the wings; flute hints the ancient capabilities of the soul.
Promising, yet does not instruct how.
Teasing, teasing.

Body and soul resonate in perfect balance.
Human and music join,
becoming one.

- - -

What I experienced listening to one particular music piece. This is in the now retired *Undefined Reality* course workbook.

- - -

Music, with or without lyrics, tells a story. I sat one day, closed my eyes and energetically followed the music. What the instruments "said" and what the whole composition spoke of was pretty awesome.

~ ~~ ~ ~~ ~

What Are You?

I am
the known and unknown.
I am
the remembered and forgotten.
I am
the never before experienced.

I am
the Watcher.
I am
the Doer.
I am
the Record Keeper.

And so are you.

– – –

Reality Undefined website: Okay, not from the past. I have been asked (for more years than I care to remember) "What Are You?"

Today I have, and share, an answer.

- - -

We are each what this poem describes – our purpose of being here and the different roles we play over our lifetime on Earth.

We each are known and unknown; the remembered and the forgotten, and so much more. And what it all boils down to is that we each are "I AM".

~ ~~ ~ ~~ ~

Do They Matter?

The dreams I had
of yesteryear –
and the dreams I
had last night.

Are they real or
imagined?
Or does it matter
if I learn?

- - -

I pretty much question just about everything – including my own dreams.

Dreams help guide us, train us, remind us, or show us what's going on in our lives.

Do I need to pay attention? Do any of us? My answer, for me, is yes.

~ ~~ ~ ~~ ~

The Illusion of Self

Illusion discovered
the cracks had begun
What lays beneath them?
Afraid to know.

The illusion of self –
had held for so long –
shattered into a
million pieces.

Anger and tears arise –
vying for the spot.
Validation please
of self long past.

Fractured beyond; no two
pieces the same size.
Small and large alike
reflecting…who?

It's time to begin now…
the journey anew.
Leaving shards behind –
and look within.

For the answer we seek
comes from within us –
Not from someone else.
Get to *know* self.

\- - -

Reality Undefined website

- - -

We each accepted labels and parameters of self given to us from others.

When one starts questioning who they really are, the work can begin…starting with the shattering of the illusions of labels and parameters of who we are based on what we accepted from others throughout our life.

Who are you really?

~ ~~ ~ ~~ ~

And Some Dance With Delight

As time progresses, I see the patterns
that people are weaving for
their lives.

We each dance and move; we mold and
create with the energy to make our own
tomorrows.

Some are not so pleasantly surprised
when their self-created tomorrows
come...

And some dance with delight.

We really are the creators of our reality. If you are disappointed by your creation, you are welcome and encouraged to create something else.

~ ~~ ~ ~~ ~

Once More

Every morning I awaken to music –
sweet etheric, not from here
music.

Music that calls to my core –
the very essence of my
being.

A feeling of familiarity –
slightly out of reach – aches within
me.

The day breaks – I cover my head
hoping to stay and keep
listening…

But the day intrudes and pushes the
calming heavenly tunes
away.

So each night I hope that I will awaken
in the morning to those beautiful
sounds…

Once more.

- - -

Reality Undefined website

- - -

Off and on, since I was a kid, I heard music from beyond; music that cannot be reproduced by us, humans. Music so sweet and beautiful, its harmony soothes the soul and reminds us of where we came from before Earth.

My being aches to hear it again.

~ ~~ ~ ~~ ~

Kindred Soul

When I look into your eyes, I see that you are who you are –
there are no pretenses – no lying about who you are.

I see sorrow for the Earth and its inhabitants
I see hope for Earth and its inhabitants

I see peace and energetic beauty

I see a desire for harmony throughout all

I see you to the depth of your soul
I see a Kindred Soul

And I thank you for being who you are
and being in my life.

- - -

Reality Undefined website

- - -

Growing up, I felt so alone because of my abilities and of how I saw the world and its inhabitants.

As I matured, I began seeing sparks in some people's eyes; and eventually began finding and seeing Kindred Souls.

Today, there are so many spiritually awakened people on Earth that I no longer feel so alone.

Thank you.

~ ~~ ~ ~~ ~

Soon

Stretching, twisting, rubbing…
anything to get the old, heavy third dimensional energy off.

Glimpses of crystalline shining through empty spots that
used to be carbon-based.

The etheric voices and music touching me more and more –
teasing with promises of more when the old has gone.

Bright flashes of white Light;
Winged creatures unknown on 3rd.
The "calling" pulling at my heart,
driving me towards higher and higher frequencies.

My 3rd dimensional body is so tired –
aching to release itself to the crystalline -
the struggle to be finished -
3rd gone & fully into the 5th.

Soon…

Soon.

- - -

Reality Undefined website: Trying to put into words the feeling of releasing the heavier more dense energies to allow the lighter ~ and my impatience with how long it seems to be taking.

- - -

I felt, going through these growth times, like I was a piece of taffy being pulled, twisted, wrung and pulled again.

~ ~~ ~ ~~ ~

An Illusion

As I watch, I see my
third dimensional world crumbling around me.

Many deaths
severed connections
distancing friends

I feel alone; I feel lonely

I panic in the Silence around me.

I grieve the loss of my third dimensional world.

Within, I see such bright beauty becoming my new reality.

Many rebirths
new connections
friends close

The feeling of being alone was but an illusion.

In the Silence is the Truth.

I welcome my joining with the fifth dimension…

I am ready.

I Am.

- - -

Reality Undefined website: I tried to put into prose what I and some others may been feeling and/or experiencing lately.

- - -

As we grow spiritually, we have many friends who leave us because our energies are no longer harmonious with theirs. It can be a difficult transition, but there are others who resonate with the new frequency we carry – who are ready to enter our life.

~ ~~ ~ ~~ ~

Distant Tears

I hear the sound of
distant tears

falling so far away.

The doubt, the fears
and loneliness

of being so far away.

I ask that you do
not despair…

you are only a thought away.

No regrets, or second
guessing –

they only get in the way.

Stand tall and then
step forward –

only your thoughts stand in your way.

Nothing lost – much
to gain…

For this is the way

to growth, love and
inner peace…

they are not that far away.

- - -

Reality Undefined website: Sometimes I can hear someone softly crying in the distance – or feel tears of anguish slide down someone's face as they cry.

- - -

As an empath, I can sometimes Feel other's emotions, especially the heavier ones. I energetically sit with them and offer Light to help them on their journey. And when they are joyous, my heart sings for them.

~ ~~ ~ ~~ ~

Spectator Sport

They gather around
excited to bear witness
to this game.

Whispering, speculating
perhaps betting on
what happens next….

in this Spectator Sport.

More and more arrive
even some re-uniting
going on…

All while the "star" sits;
watching, thinking and
waiting.

Some spectators try
to get messages to
the star…

Hoping to be seen,
recognized, heard and
perhaps helped.

The spectators are: specters;
wise one's of old; loved ones
and visitors…

All coming to see
as the events unfold
on Earth.

This particular game is
ongoing…daily…
It is my life.

I am the “star”

Of this Spectators Sport.

- - -

Reality Undefined website: We each walk daily, with our support Team and visitors with us – sometimes making us feel like the “star attraction” in this…your game of life.

- - -

One thing about being able to see “Other” is that I can see beings who gather to watch and learn from those of us on Earth.

I usually See it when I sit with one or more Lightworkers (generic term here). I See us sitting at the bottom of an arena and the viewing seats are packed by beings from everywhere.

I once asked my Team about it and they explained that those who were not brave enough, or had no desire, to have a human experience would/will often gather to learn through the conversations, hands on experiences, and questions presented of those who are having the physical Earth experience.

We, humans, are the stars of this Spectator Sport.

~ ~~ ~ ~~ ~

Something Happened Last Night

Something happened last night;
I feel changed somehow.

The weather kept waking me
after I went to bed

So it wasn't a solid sleep...
I tossed and turned, too.

Something happened last night
and I feel changed somehow.

I tried to meditate today
to find an answer...

but the howling winds
distracted me again and again.

Yet something happened last night
and I feel changed somehow.

So I guess I'll just have to wait and see...

- - -

Reality Undefined website: Ever wake up and feel that you changed overnight? Like something – positive – altered in you, but you can't quite put your finger on it? Hmmm....

~ ~~ ~ ~~ ~

Break Free!

Dreams stir within
the heaviness which
laden the subconscious.
Blood cells carry our
ancestor's memories –
Etheric separated
from physical. The
barrier? Our own ignorance.

Days pass, cycles continue
galaxy wide –
Yet we remain within
individual cocoons,
waiting for someone
else to set us free.

Teachers teach –
Preachers preach –
and both are
meaningless echoes,
unable to penetrate
our self-induced
existence.

- - -

Retired *Undefined Reality* course workbook & Reality Undefined website.

- - -

We can tap into so much more than we currently do; but many of us willingly keep the blinders on. We are so much more than the labels and programming we accepted from others; we accepted because we consciously did not know better because we were young.

As adults, it becomes our own ignorance that keeps us from being our full, true selves.

~ ~~ ~ ~~ ~

Empath Overload

The anguish builds –

the tears
the fears
the regrets

of thousands of other people…
echoing in my head.

They cannot latch onto me
but I can hear/sense
all that they contain.

And waves of their heavy
sorrowful energies crash against
my barriers

Seeking somewhere to latch on.

– – –

Our emotions – the emotions of over 7 billion people on Earth – can be overwhelming for an empath – even when we erect a shield to buffer us. We can still Sense, Feel, and/or Hear the emotions.

An empath feels other's emotions as strongly as their own. Other's pain, fear, worry, sorrow, etc. feels very heavy, as though the empath alone is shouldering them.

Yet, when others are rejoicing, excited, happy…these emotions lift the empath as though it was their own happiness.

During the Covid years, people's fear, anxiety, worries, uncertainties, depression, and terror felt like I was being smothered. These emotions were being generated world-wide and all at the same time; this made the energies of the emotions a large unhealthy energy generator.

~ ~~ ~ ~~ ~

We Are One

The spiraling time
has no beginning,
has no end.

Tomorrows are now
as are yesterdays
and todays.

I AM is spread out
throughout time found on
the spiral.

She, he, both, neither.
Delineation
blurring now.

Everything is but
energy. Us too.
So it's true.

You, me, he, she are
all the same. We are
the I AM.

We Are One.

- - -

Reality Undefined website

- - -

Though we feel separate and feel like we're traveling a linear time line, we are not. We are not separate, and time is not linear. Everything's happening now and we are all One.

~ ~~ ~ ~~ ~

Metaphysical 2

Having an Empath as a Friend

Though miles may separate us
the bond never broke.

Over the years, I have felt your tears
and cried with you.

I held you when you were
wracked with misery.

I stood beside you through
your confusion.

I felt your loneliness,
fears and your pain.

My heart clenched
with your anguish.

And rejoiced when you began
removing the chains.

I cheered as you tested
your wings once again.

I never left you and
have talked to you daily.

My soul soared with joy
when your soul soared.

Isn't that what friends are for, even
when we may be miles apart?

The soul knows no distance
or boundary, ever.

- - -

Reality Undefined website: Having an empath as a friend.

- - -

A friend in a distant state was emotionally distraught – and I felt it every day for three years. This person energetically visited me every evening for three years until s/he was able to say, "Enough!" and change the direction of their life.

~ ~~ ~ ~~ ~

May Light Pave Your Way

You come to me
in your dreams -
seeking solace
from your torments.

Your frustrations, fears
and loneliness
ripple across
the dimensions.

Your tears spill
on my floor.

And I can only offer
a soft palliative.
I cannot take this
pain from you,

for it is of your
own making.

Only when you
awaken to your
truth and release
past patterns…

…will your healing
begin.

May you be guided
from your nightmares

and may Light
pave your way.

- - -

Reality Undefined website: This poem or prose talks about the times those in distress may energetically (or astrally) visit me or someone who aided them in the past.

Embarrassment or shame (for whatever reason), fear of rejection (again, for whatever reason), depression, or fear in general may be some of the reasons why they seek one out astrally instead of physically.

We can't take another's pain for them, nor can we make the changes for them; we can offer suggestions or support for their journey.

~ ~~ ~ ~~ ~

Sometimes

Sometimes others' grief is too heavy.

Sometimes others' anger is too abrasive.

Sometimes others' fear is overwhelming.

Sometimes I feel too much.

Sometimes I know too much.

Sometimes I hear too much.

Sometimes it's painful to see so much.

Sometimes being an empath hurts too much.

Sometimes I feel so small against all of those big energies.

Sometimes I want to hide from the world's negative experience energies.

Sometimes I ache for the peace of my true home.

But, most times I feel so blessed to be in the midst of all of this and helping others.

- - -

In *Prophecy Revealed*

This was written for Book 2 of the World Paranormal Organization series, *Prophecy Revealed: Clarima Syd Jones* describing what it can feel like sometimes, being an empath.

~ ~~ ~ ~~ ~

Pain, Love & Everything In Between

I remember childhood innocence.
I hate how it was ripped from me.

I remember the long road
to trust again.

I remember life
before "Jan"

And had glimpses of
life after "Jan".

I remember death
and destruction

and I remember
pure paradise and harmony.

In a blink of an eye, flashes from
this life and others sped by.

In the space between each
inhale and exhale, I find peace.

I learned to appreciate how
I arrived here today.

Pain, love and everything
in between.

I have been the giver.
I have been the receiver

of pain, love and everything
in between.

- - -

Who we are today is a compilation of our experiences and reactions or actions of this lifetime and other lifetimes.

It is not the experiences that define who you become – it's the reaction to the experience. Did you react and move into victim-mode? Did you stay there? Or did you learn from the experience and move on?

~ ~~ ~ ~~ ~

Forever Trapped in 3D

"I am done!"

I screamed to the sky.

The cold squared buildings
witnessed my proclamation.

"I've had it with those who
refuse to accept responsibility
for their own actions!"

I yelled to the smelly
tar parking lot.

"I don't want anything
more to do with 3D!"

I spit out through gritted teeth.

My husband saw the frustration
and pain in my eyes,
he opened his arms…

And folded them around me…
as I cried.

"I'm done with 3D," I said into
his chest. "I hate the third dimension."

He held me until I cried
out my frustrations.

He pulled back and examined
my face. "Better?" he asked.

Face blotchy from ugly crying, I nodded.
“I still don’t like 3D,” I muttered.

“Let’s go get some dinner.”

We walked off towards
the restaurant.

I wonder what the buildings
and tarred parking lot thought
of my outburst…

for they are forever trapped
in 3D.

- - -

Yeah, I had a meltdown one day. I’d been dealing with companies on the phone for hours and had my fill of the games people operating in the third dimension energy play. Yuck!

~ ~~ ~ ~~ ~

Every Aspect of Being Human

Memories echo in the corridors
of my mind.

Memories of so many places
and times

on Earth and
Elsewhere.

Sometimes the echoes
are loud;

sometimes they are
gentle.

Some are horrific;
some of love.

Lack, fear, hate,
greed and loathing.

Of love, peace, compassion
and kindness.

Powerful and helplessness.
Serene and combustible.

Squalor and luxuriousness.
Warrior and monk.

We each have traveled time,
working to experience

every aspect of being
human.

So what are you going to do with
all of these experiences?

- - -

My belief is that we each have had multiple lifetimes – both on and off Earth.

Some people are Earth Regulars – those who just keep coming back to Earth.

Some are only here during transformative times for the human race.

Regardless of how many lifetimes on Earth, we each work to not only experience every aspect of being a human, but also to heal traumas we endured in this lifetime and our other lifetimes. That's what we're doing in this lifetime, whether one is consciously aware of it or not.

~ ~~ ~ ~~ ~

In That One Moment

I sat at a red light. I looked around at the
vehicles and saw people

with no faces.

Like something from a science
fiction movie.

Panic started to bubble up.

I took a deep breath
and asked my Team,

"What am I seeing?"

Individual expressions
of self; of One.

In that one moment, I felt:

Expansiveness and
connection to All.

In that one moment, I knew:

They are all me & I am
each of them.

One.

- - -

Every once and a while I have these experiences of feeling the connection of All.

Sometimes, I can have this insight or Knowing while sitting at a stop light; sometimes it's in that one moment between sleep and awake.

It's not very often...just an occasional and gentle reminder that separatism is nothing but an illusion; a powerful one, but illusion nonetheless.

~ ~~ ~ ~~ ~

I Bend a Knee to No Man

I bend a knee to no man.

Expectancy hung heavy
in the air of the old church.

The pews were mostly empty
this Wednesday afternoon.

I, as a child, was seated with my grandmother
as we watched the priest walk in.

The few people stood as the priest
raised his hands and spoke.

Dark tendrils emanated from him and
reached out to the congregation.

The air shifted as the
congregation rote replied.

Those who called out a response
were wrapped in one of those tendrils.

I understood none of the Latin words
but I did understand the energy and intent.

Grandmother motioned for me
as to when to stand, sit or kneel.

I bend a knee to no man.

Afterwards, the priest shook everyone's hands,
thus locking the dark tendrils in place…

…deep into each church member.

I bend a knee to no man.

In the parking lot, I peppered my
grandmother with questions.

The biggest one was, "Did you understand
what the priest was saying?"

"No," she replied, "it was in Latin."

"Then how do you know
what you're agreeing to?"

She stopped mid-stride, "We do not
question the Church!"

"Even if you don't know what
they're saying?" I persisted.

I was never invited back.

This was an unsettling experience with the Catholic Church; but it wasn't my only experience.

When I was in the third grade, the school had placed a T-building (temporary building) in the school parking lot. We were each sent home with a permission slip for this experimental program for CCD (Confraternity of Christian Doctrine). My mother, who had been raised strict Roman Catholic turned Protestant to marry my father, happily signed.

I climbed the steps and opened the door. What comes next is what I can remember of my CCD experience.

The walls were painted blood red above the chair rail. The chair rail held little statues, while the walls were covered in prayer cards and pictures of Mother Mary, Jesus' crucifixion, Jesus and the Apostles, etc. This initial presentation was scary to me.

Desks were lined up neatly facing the teacher's desk, which was tucked in a little alcove.

I stifled a surprised nervous giggle as an angry looking woman stepped out. Never having seen a nun before, I questioned why she was dressed like a penguin.

The nun's first lesson was about how everyone who is not Catholic will burn in hell forever. I raised my hand.

"What?" she snapped.

"So anyone not Catholic gets sent to hell?"

"Yes."

"But wasn't Jesus Jewish?" I asked.

"We do not question the Church!" Punishment was swift as the hard ruler slammed down across my knuckles.

The next CCD class was on the 2nd commandment, "Thou shall not make unto thee any graven image." The nun explained that it meant that we aren't allowed to make and worship any idols.

I raised my hand.

She rolled her eyes, "What?"

I pointed to the statues and to the imagery on the walls. "But those are graven images then, right?"

The ruler was whipped out and slammed against my knuckles.

When I got off the bus that afternoon, my mother was standing on the front stoop screaming at me. I was too far away to understand what she was saying.

As I moved closer to her, I heard, "How could you do this to me? How could you embarrass me that way? What is wrong with you?" and other accusatory comments. I hadn't a clue how I managed to tick her off without having been at home.

When I reached the stoop, she angrily explained that the Archbishop called and told her that I was banned from CCD.

I was okay with that. My Catholic raised and schooled mother was not.

Being able to See/Feel and interpret energy, for me, I feel that my connection with the Source does not need to be controlled, manipulated or filtered through someone who feels they speak on behalf of the Source and does not allow questions to be asked and explored. And these two examples were what drove this home for me at a young age.

~ ~~ ~ ~~ ~

Hidden in Plain Sight

I was excited as the light
filled my room.

This meant I got to see "them" –
those who knew and got me.

I don't remember the ride up –
but I remember being welcomed.

I walked the corridors, smiling at others
as I headed for my favorite spot…

The arboretum in the
center of the ship.

There I greeted old friends
and made new ones.

These beings understood me
as humans could not.

Here I felt home. I am with them,
but not one of them.

The visits were often as a
child – they kept me sane.

As I grew, the visits became
less and less.

As an adult, using my
Other Sight, I See...

They and others have been
hidden in plain sight.

Above the Earth...
camouflaged,

but always there
with us.

\- - -

I have had non-Earth beings, aka "aliens", in my life for as long as I can remember – and I feel their presence kept me sane when I was growing up; protected me from the harshness of being me on this Earth.

The sky has, to me, always contained numerous ships of all kinds – just hanging out above Earth, and hidden in, and from, plain sight.

~ ~~ ~ ~~ ~

Chaos and Order Collided

Chaos and order
collided at lunch.

He callously ripped a hole
in the dimensional fabric;

The ragged edges flapped
in the etheric wind.

A glimpse into another
dimension – stars unfamiliar.

"Why?" I asked. "Why do you
rip the dimensional fabric?"

He smirked. His arrogance dripped
from his words, "Because I can."

His energy spoke of how he
reveled in the chaos he created.

"Why are you so concerned about
what I do?" he demanded.

"Because I have to clean up
after your carelessness."

He waved a dismissive hand towards me.
"Then you'll be busy a long time."

I lost my appetite and could no
longer sit with chaos.

- - -

I have met many people and beings over my lifetime. The ones who chafe me are those who are so cavalier about their destructive words or actions and don't care in the least of how it will affect others.

It just so happened that this guy created chaos on a larger scale, affecting not only those on Earth, but life everywhere.

~ ~~ ~ ~~ ~

The Trap

Taking your first breath
begins the indoctrination.

Rules, regulations and boundaries
shoved at you left and right.

Obey or receive punishment…
Is that free will?

As an adult, choices are
made on a daily basis.

Which rule do I comply with and
which rule do I push against?

The battle continues
throughout this lifetime.

Glimpses of past lives
occasionally show themselves.

Yes, we all had other lives
on this large so-called spinning blue marble.

As we age, we are no longer
so concerned about complying…

often skirting the unspoken
rules and protocols.

Upon our last breath –
we go to the Light…

The Trap

to keep you in the
reincarnation cycle.

Rinse and repeat.

Continuing to feed
the system…

The Trap…

that keeps you bound
to the endless cycle.

How to escape

The Trap?

Don't go into the white Light –
go to the Blue Portal

and tell it you want
to go home…

your true home,
and out of The Trap.

It's time to end the cycle.

- - -

We have complied and re-entered the reincarnation cycle, aka "The Trap" over and over again.

The Trap has been exposed, and now we fight against it to end the cycle. It's time for us to go back to our true home – to see our loved ones at our origination point.

Earth life experience was supposed to be temporary – not endless loops, keeping The Trap's system fed and powered.

When this body ceases to function, go home...your real and true home.

~ ~~ ~ ~~ ~

I Do Not Guard My Tongue

I have awakened the
truth-seeker within,

which awakened the
truth-speaker within.

I do not guard my tongue,
but speak my truths.

Take it or leave it –
your choice.

- - -

When you have awakened the truth seeker with in you, holding your tongue – or not speaking your truths – becomes difficult. Speaking one's truth needn't be aggressive, pushy or expressed at inappropriate times. It can be expressed in many ways – find a way that works for you.

~ ~~ ~ ~~ ~

I Remember My Light

I've looked into the
soulless eyes of another.

I've seen evil – both
human and non-human.

I've seen some
influenced by evil.

I've seen
my duality.

And I remember my Light.

I've seen the Light
in the eyes of others.

I've seen
pure consciousness.

I've seen some influenced
by beautiful white Light.

I've accepted my duality.

I remember my Light.

Do you?

- - -

We are here to experience duality and to find our way back to the Source (or whatever you may call it). We see, experience and get to know both sides; but it's up to each one of us as to what side we want to dwell in.

One of the first things we need to find our way back is to remember our own light; it's always been within us...we just forgot.

~ ~~ ~ ~~ ~

Curse Breakers

We carry our ancestor's memories within
our own blood cells.

Generations of trauma; of hopes; of
loss and of dreams.

Their blood cells recorded their experiences –
and passed those memories down through time.

We carry their cellular memories
in our own cells.

Is this why addictions or abuse can
"run" in family lines?

Is this why we can remember things
we've never experienced?

Because our cells remember
our ancestors experiences?

Is this what we're cleaning up
in our ancestral line?

We are the generational curse breakers.

- - -

Energetically speaking, we do carry our ancestors' experience memories – positive or negative – in our own blood cells. Our blood remembers what our ancestors endured; it remembers and it passes along the information on to the next generation.

Many of us here now have come to energetically clean up our ancestral line; to break the cycle of that which was passed on before us. It can stop with each one of us...or are you going to perpetuate it?

~ ~~ ~ ~~ ~

The Keeper of Your Ancestors

Does a "myth" feel like it
was real to you?

Do the cellular memories of your distant
relatives whisper to you…

reminding you of co-existing
with dragons?

Of drinking spring waters blessed
by a unicorn's horn?

Of watching mere-folk playing and
splashing in the waters?

What if the myths of today
are yesteryear's truth?

Our "recorded" history has been altered,
deleted, redacted and censured.

But your blood cells – the keeper of
your ancestors – remembers it all.

Generations upon generations of memories
are passed down through the blood line.

The stories of yesteryears are memories;
truths forgotten or hidden from us today.

You are the memory keeper
of your vast array of ancestors.

- - -

I grew up remembering places and times of mythological beings. I remember interactions with dragons, unicorns and more.

It never felt like fantasy to me. The Knowing had always been in my mind; memories of other times and places. Beings relegated to stories passed down.

I Knew they weren't just stories because my memories were too detailed…or were they memories of my ancestors of times forgotten?

~ ~~ ~ ~~ ~

I Hear Them

I sometimes wonder if it's worth it –
does it make any difference?

I pull back and slide into neutral –
idling while I ponder.

Then, in the space between
the inhale and the exhale,

I Hear them.

Those who came before me and
those who come after me.

They tell me that, because of me,
they are free – no longer tethered.

They show me the cord
linking past to the future.

The cord that kept them
stuck in the old energies.

I Hear them

as they say

that my work, my hopes, my love
is what set them – and me – free.

Just because I don't physically see it
doesn't mean it hasn't helped.

I Hear them

still

encouraging me to keep going –
as they send me love and support.

So, yeah, it's worth it.

- - -

Every person has moments of doubt about their life at one point or another.

Faith, to me, is the trust and belief in what you cannot see. But even those with Other Senses may falter in the faith of what we do.

But our loved ones – our ancestors and descendants – send us love and encouragement to keep going…to have faith that, on some level, our work matters and does make a difference, even if we can't see it.

Keep going, and thank you.

~ ~~ ~ ~~ ~

In Conclusion

Though I began with working to express myself – as a form of release – through poetry, prose and short stories, my writing expanded into writing articles for my website, Reality Undefined at metaphysical-studies.com

It was my intent, via my website, to offer a place for others to explore the metaphysical, spiritual and paranormal. I shared my experiences and interpretations over the years hoping it would help others not feel so alone on their life's journey.

Thank you for reading this and may it aid you on your life journey.

Jan

About the Author

Jan Toomer resides with her husband in the desert Southwest in the United States. Jan is a writer and author; a Metaphysical, Spiritual and Paranormal Consultant; Reiki Master; creator of New Dimension Energy Session; as well as Founder and Owner of Reality Undefined LLC.

Born a multi-talented sensitive, Jan has literally been doing energy work for most of her life. Some of her abilities are energy healing, medium and channeler, animal communicator, energy reader and interpreter.

She also studied Metaphysics, Ho'oponopono and the Akashic Records.

She aids others to see a different perspective to help expand their awareness and consciousness; to bring reality-creating consciously into their lives.

Jan writes and freely shares a her articles, since 2008, on Metaphysical, Spiritual and Paranormal topics for her blog Reality Undefined at https://www.metaphysical-studies.com/ and does videos on YouTube (@jantoomer3828) as well.

Acknowledgements

It's always a joy hearing what Mary Smith has to say about my books. A big thank you to fellow author, Mary Smith, for her support and encouragement, and for letting me bounce ideas back and forth.

My Hubby for his patience and support for my need to write and encouragement for me to continue.

And to all of my friends who put up with my writing days.

Also by Jan Toomer

Cursed Dagger and Dragon: Clarima Syd Jones

This is the first book in the World Paranormal Organization series.

Clarima "Clari" Jones, ranked a Level IV Energy Reader with the World Paranormal Organization, is a paranormal consultant that uses her abilities not only in her private practice, but also to aid the local PD's cold cases with Detective Morris.

The realm of other dimensions is physically introduced to Clari and Det. Morris, and they find themselves in a small war where Clari calls on the aid of the dragons and Other Beings.

But lately things have gotten a little personal. Someone tried to kill Clari and almost succeeded. Clari finds out the Grigori are also after her, and she has no idea why any of this is happening, but with the help of her friends, she's determined to find out.

Available on Amazon

– – – – –

Prophecy Revealed: Clarima Syd Jones

This is the second book in the World Paranormal Organization series.

The story continues with Morris recovering in the hospital while the World Paranormal Organization's investigation is ongoing to determine Clari's part in the death of a Grigori.

Since Clari neglected to tell the World Paranormal Organization about her other abilities, the WPO suspended Clari's certification until she retested with them. When the testing concluded, Clari began training to control her other abilities. One of the training sessions was for her to learn how to control her dragon aspect; but this led to Clari inciting a revolution in the Dragon Realm.

With Detective Morris released from the hospital, Clari digs deeper into why the Grigori want her dead. Clari is informed about the Avatar Prophecy, and her friends think the prophecy is talking about her.

Ghosts from the 1940's ask Clari for help in crossing over; they are trapped. She and Morris begin looking into each individual ghost's story to see what the commonality is and how to help them.

After yet another attempt on her life, Clari discovers that not only are the Grigori connections close to home, but also that the Grigori are more widespread than anyone thought.

Can she put all the pieces together and expose the Grigori before another attempt on her life; an attempt that may succeed this time?

Available on Amazon

The third book in this series, focusing on Raven Danvers, coming soon.

- - - - -

Re-Writing My Future: A Stroke in Time

Jan's memoir shares her journey from growing up with active abilities while wanting her abilities removed so she could be deemed "normal". Then, as she developed a tenuous relationship with her abilities, she had a stroke in her 30's and lost touch with her abilities. She struggled to not only find her new "norm", but to get her abilities back while she explores the question, "Who am I now?"

Jan shares her experiences and offer some insights from her own journey in hopes that her story may they help you through yours. This book for stroke survivors, caretakers of survivors, those interested in the paranormal, spiritual and metaphysical, as well as anyone who has or is facing major changes in their life.

www.ingramcontent.com/pod-product-compliance
Lightning Source LLC
LaVergne TN
LVHW050629100826
845148LV00011B/1796

9798986681276